MORAH, MORAH, TEACH ME TORAH!

A Multimedia Approach to Teaching the Weekly Parashah All Year Round

Tobey Greenberg and Nechama Retting

ISBN 10: 1-934527-26-2

ISBN 13: 978-1-934527-26-9

Torah Aura Productions • 4423 Fruitland Avenue, Los Angeles, CA 90058
(800) BE-Torah • (800) 238-6724 • (323) 585-7312 • fax (323) 585-0327
E-MAIL <misrad@torahaura.com>
Visit the Torah Aura website at www.torahaura.com

Manufactured in the United States of America

ACKNOWLEDGEMENTS

Without the encouragement, support, and enthusiasm from several people, this book would not have been possible. First, we would like to thank Diane Holsten and Lisa Ginsburg-Arber, two talented Jewish educators whose creative ideas have been an inspiration in writing this book. Next, we would like to thank the many rabbis whose encouraging words and wisdom kept us writing and creating the various elements of this book. Thank you to Rabbi David Kalender, Rabbi Joshua Ben-Gideon, Rabbi Rebecca Ben-Gideon, Rabbi Stuart Marks, and Rabbi Shalom Deitsch. Other people we'd like to thank who were instrumental in contributing their help are Chanie Deitsch, Rochel Ohayon, Mendy Werdeyger (from MostlyMusic.com), Carol Boyd Leon, Irene Light, Meryl Weiner, Judith Caplan Ginsburgh, Lenny Solomon (from Shlock Rock), and all the other Jewish songwriters who have inspired us.

Of course it was the children we teach for whom this book was designed and created. It is because of their constant enthusiasm in wanting to take part in the reenactment of the Torah stories, their never-ending desire to learn more about Torah, their joy in singing the songs, and their eagerness in participating in the multimedia ideas that enhance each parashah that we wanted to create this book. Our hope is that other Jewish educators will utilize and implement into their curriculum the ideas that we successfully use daily, so that they can experience the joy of teaching Torah as we do.

Thanks to Jewish educators all over the world who give everlasting time and devotion to guiding and teaching our children respect, knowledge, and love for our Jewish heritage.

A special thank you goes to our families for their patience, support, and understanding during the creation of this book, and to Alan Papkin for being so patient and helpful with all his computer advice.

Last, but not least, thanks to Sara Citrenbaum, who created our beautiful Website that can be found at: www.Torah4kids.com.

Contents

Acknowledgements. 3
Teacher's Introduction 7
Children's Introduction 9

Bereshit 11
Noah. 23
Lekh-Lekha 29
Va-Yera 37
Hayyei Sarah. 43
Toldot 49
Va-Yetze 55
Va-Yishlah 61
Va-Yeshev 65
Miketz 71
Va-Yigash 75
Va-Yehi. 79

Shemot 83
Va-Era 87
Bo 91
Beshallah 97
Yitro 103
Mishpatim 109
Terumah 113
Tetzaveh 119
Ki Tissa. 123
Va-Yak'hel 127
Pekudei 133

Va-Yikra. 137
Tzav 141

Shemini . . . 145
Tazria . . . 149
Metzora . . . 153
Aharei Mot . . . 161
Kedoshim . . . 165
Emor . . . 169
Be-Har . . . 173
Be-Hukkotai . . . 177

Be-Midbar . . . 181
Naso . . . 185
Be-Ha'alotekha . . . 189
Shelah-Lekha . . . 193
Korah . . . 199
Hukkat . . . 203
Balak . . . 207
Pinhas . . . 211
Mattot . . . 215
Mas'ei . . . 219

Devarim . . . 223
Va-Ethannan . . . 229
Ekev . . . 233
Re'eh . . . 237
Shoftim . . . 243
Ki Tetze . . . 247
Ki Tavo . . . 251
Nitzavim . . . 257
Va-Yelekh . . . 261
Ha'azinu . . . 265
V'zot Ha-Brakhah . . . 269
Rosh Hodesh . . . 273
Bibliography . . . 277
Music Resources . . . 278
About the Authors . . . 279

TEACHER'S INTRODUCTION

Each week a chapter (or parashah) of the Torah is read. The goal of this book is to teach young children (and their families) about each of these parashiyot through the use of drama, stories, music, crafts, science, math, language, and cooking. We suggest creating a parashah prop box. In it you might include dress-up clothing (an easy outfit can be made from a pillow case with a slit up the center and armholes cut out), belts, scarves, various kippot, crowns, fake beards, fake fur, puppets, animal masks, and so on. In our school, we utilize a variety of multimedia ideas to enhance and bring the Torah alive during our interactive *Kabbalat Shabbat* programs. Try to create a special time and a special place in the classroom or synagogue to tell the stories from the Torah. We like to make every Friday a unique and special day: we take out toys that we don't play with during the week, we take out the Shabbat kit for the family corner, and we cover the tables with white tablecloths, to name just a few ideas. We also suggest you make a floor map of Israel (see Parashat Mas'ei) to use during your weekly Torah time.

This book includes songs that relate to most parashiyot. We did our best to find the authors to all the songs. If we have inadvertently not credited an artist correctly, please forgive us and let us know, so we may credit you in future printings. Unless otherwise noted, the lyrics to these songs have been created by the authors, using traditional, familiar tunes hopefully we all know. The songs written by the authors can be downloaded for free on our website www.Torah4kids.com.

Creating a mural on large butcher paper (or 8½ x 14-inch paper and rolled onto paper towel rolls) depicting the scenes of each parashah is a great way to reinforce the stories. Each week you could have your children create a new picture depicting the parashah to add to the mural, and by the end of the year you will have your very own Torah created by your students.

We have used the word "God" instead of "Hashem" and indicated other Hebrew biblical names, but everyone should use the words they are comfortable with. This book contains God's name. Please treat it with respect.

Parentheses ( ) are used to indicate teacher-directed activities. We hope you will use these ideas at school and at home to enrich your children's learning experiences.

At the end of each parashah we have created family discussion pages with discussion questions that can be photocopied and sent home to parents. The questions are appropriate for Shabbat dinner discussions. We also suggest the use of "Ask Me" stickers during the week leading up to *Kabbalat Shabbat*. After learning together, send the children home wearing a sticker with a visual prompt for discussion (you could also e-mail the parents and tell them what you learned about). Example: For *Bereshit*, send children home wearing "Ask me what God created on *Yom Rishon*."

It is customary to dip children's fingers in honey and place them on Hebrew letters, emphasize the sweetness of learning. So, enjoy some sweet nosh your first time learning Torah together. And, remember to say the *brakhah* before beginning:

בָּרוּךְ אַתָּה יי אֱלֹהֵינוּ מֶלֶךְ הָעוֹלָם אֲשֶׁר קִדְּשָׁנוּ בְּמִצְוֹתָיו וְצִוָּנוּ לַעֲסוֹק בְּדִבְרֵי תוֹרָה.

Barukh Attah Adonai Eloheinu Melekh ha-Olam asher kid'shanu b'mitzvotav v'tzivanu la'asok b'divrei Torah.

Blessed are You, Eternal, our God, Ruler of the Cosmos, Who makes us holy with commandments and commands us to study Torah.

CHILDREN'S INTRODUCTION

The Torah is a really good book, the kind of book that we want to read over and over again because we like to learn what it teaches us. How is this book different from other books you read? There are lots of stories about the Jewish people in the Torah, which we read every Shabbat. We can also read the Torah on Mondays, on Thursdays, on Rosh Hodesh, and on some holidays. Each story, or chapter, is called a parashah, and there are fifty-four parashiyot in the whole Torah. The parashiyot are grouped together into the Five Books of Moshe (Moses), and those five books compiled together make one Torah scroll. Here is a song about the five books of the Torah:

SONG (tune: *Adon Olam*—traditional/repetitive version, with adaptations by the authors)

Oh there are five [shout out "five" and put out your hand] books of the Torah
Oh there are five (five) books that we read
Oh there are five (five) books of the Torah
We read five books of Torah each and every year.

First is BERESHIT, then we read SHEMOT
And then we read the book of VA-YIKRA
Then comes BE-MIDBAR, and last is DEVARIM
And then we start all over and we read it again.

Oh there are five (five) books of the Torah
Oh there are five (five) books that we read
Oh there are five (five) books of the Torah
We read five books of Torah each and every year.

BERESHIT

There is so much that happens in this parashah! We have chosen to cover just creation and the Garden of Eden. The story of Cain and Abel is also a great story to learn. Therefore, we suggest some additional books at the end of the chapter to enhance your learning.

Bereshit means "in the beginning." In the beginning there was nothing. What do you think it means for there to be nothing? (See what your children come up with!) There was only God. Everything was dark. God created the whole world in only six days! Can you imagine, a whole world created in only six days? On the seventh day God finished the work (*avodah*) and rested (*m'nuhah*).

YOM RISHON—Sunday

On day number one, God looked around and said, "Let there be light." And there was light. Now there was a separation between the darkness and the light. God saw that the separation was good. God called the darkness night, and the light day. There was evening and there was morning, the first day.

YOM SHEINI—Monday

On day number two, God said, "Let there be a space between the waters." God called the space sky. God saw that this was good. And there was evening and there was morning, the second day.

YOM SH'LISHI—Tuesday

On day number three, God said, "Let the waters below gather together into one area and let the dry land appear. Let the land be called Earth and let the Earth grow plants and trees of every kind." God saw that this was good. And there was evening and there was morning, the third day.

YOM R'VI'I—Wednesday

On day number four, God said, "Let there be lights in the sky. The moon and stars to shine by night, and the sun, by day." God saw that this was good. And there was evening and there was morning, the fourth day.

YOM HAMISHI—Thursday

On day number five, God said, "Let there be fish and sea creatures of all kinds to fill the waters, and birds to fly in the sky." God saw that this was good. And there was evening and there was morning, the fifth day.

YOM SHISHI—Friday

On day number six, God created animals of every kind—lions, bears, skunks, snakes, monkeys, giraffes, and bugs. God saw that this was good. And God said, "I will create people to rule over the Earth and all of the animals." And God took clay from the earth's four corners and blew into it the breath of life." God named the man Adam [meaning "of the ground"]. God said to Adam, "I give to you this beautiful garden. You may eat from any tree in the garden except from the Tree of Knowledge of Good and Evil." So that Adam would not be lonely, God created a woman to keep Adam company and named her Eve (*Hava*). God created the man and woman in God's image (*b'tzelem Elohim*) and God blessed them. God told them to fill the earth and rule the animals. God saw that this was very good. And there was evening and there was morning, the sixth day.

YOM SHABBAT—Saturday

God liked all that had been created in the world. God's work was finished. God blessed this day and made it holy, and then God rested.

MULTIMEDIA IDEAS

COLORING: Coloring pages for every parashah are available at www.aish.com. Click on Torah Portion, then click on Coloring Pages.

"ASK ME" STICKER: Using computer mailing labels, think of a question to send your children home wearing to prompt family discussion: Example: "Ask me the name of the first person God created." Feel free to email parents the answers too! ☺

DAY ONE

DRAMATIC PLAY: Have a pajama party. Read bedtime stories (e.g. *Goodnight Moon* by Margaret Wise Brown).

SCIENCE: Light and dark (shadow shape) experiments.

COOKING: Bake black-and-white cookies or sugar cookies (see recipe below). You can frost them with chocolate and vanilla frosting (recipe not included).

SUGAR COOKIES

This recipe is an easy recipe to make. The dough holds its shape and won't spread during baking. Make sure you let your oven preheat before baking. The recipe can also be cut in half. It is a stiff dough (since it holds it shape), so using an electric mixer is advised.

6 cups flour	2 eggs
3 teaspoons baking powder	2 teaspoons vanilla extract
2 cups butter	1/4 teaspoons salt
2 cups sugar	

1. In an electric mixer, cream together the butter and sugar. Add eggs and vanilla. Add dry ingredients and mix well. The dough can be refrigerated.
2. Roll to desired thickness and cut into desired shapes. Bake on ungreased baking sheet at 350 degrees for 8 to 10 minutes or until just beginning to turn brown around the edges. This recipe can make up to eight dozen 3-inch cookies.

DAY TWO

SCIENCE: Do water experiments: sink and float.

Observe the clouds outside.

BOOKS: *It Looked Like Spilt Milk* by Charles G. Shaw or *The Cloud Book* by Tomie de Paola.

CRAFT: Create cloud pictures like in the book *It Looked like Spilt Milk.* Dip string into white paint, and lay the string all around the inside of a folded piece of blue paper, leaving the end sticking out. Close the paper, and pull out the string. See what it looks like. Or just spoon blobs of white paint onto dark-colored paper, fold, then open, and see what you get.

DAY THREE

SCIENCE: Take a nature walk; plant seeds.

COOKING: Make edible flowers with Twizzlers and fruit roll-ups.

MATH: Have a variety of seeds available, (e.g. pumpkin, sunflower, marigold, beans) and have children place them into matching groups, or do patterning with plants or seeds. You can also make a seed mosaic picture.

DAY FOUR

COOKING: Make moon-shaped cookies.

CRAFT: Have children cut out sun, moon, and star shapes from paper. Place the cutouts on black paper and leave out in direct sunlight for several hours. See what happens!

MATH: Sun, moon, and stars patterning.

STORY: *Why the Moon Only Glows* by Dina Rosenfeld.

DAY FIVE

MATH: Count with fish crackers (Austin's Dolphin and Friends crackers are kosher OU dairy)

STORIES: *Rainbow Fish* by Marcus Pfister or *Fish is Fish* by Eric Carle.

SCIENCE: Make bird feeders. If you live near a pond, go feed the fish!

CRAFTS: Create a beautiful picture of a rainbow fish using glitter or sequins.

DAY SIX

CRAFT: Make animal masks and learn the names of the animals in Hebrew.

MOVEMENT: Act like various animals; play "Animal Action" by Greg and Steve from *Kids in Motion* CD

MATH: Sorting and patterning with animal crackers.

Horse	*Soos*	סוּס
Duck	*Barvaz*	בַּרְוָז
Cow	*Parah*	פָּרָה
Dog	*Kelev*	כֶּלֶב
Cat	*Hatool*	חָתוּל
Pig	*Hazir*	חֲזִיר

DAY SEVEN

Celebrate Shabbat through songs, stories, and art. There are many books available with Shabbat craft ideas! Practice Shabbat by learning the *brakhot* and lighting the candles. Make Shabbat special with different toys, and try to have a Shabbat set available in your family corner. (You can make a play hallah by taking three pantyhose legs stuffed with poly-fiber fill and braiding them together. Sew to close or try knotting them.) Bake hallah with your kids. It's math, science, and language all rolled (excuse the pun) into one!

HALLAH

2 packages of yeast (2¼ teaspoons yeast per pack)
3 tablespoons sugar
4 tablespoons flour
¾ cup warm water

1. Preheat the oven to 350 degrees. Combine ingredients in a bowl and set aside to "proof." If the mixture bubbles, the yeast is active and the mixture is "proofed." If it does not bubble, the yeast is no good and you need to start over with new yeast.

6 (sometimes more) cups of flour
3 eggs
A pinch of salt
½ cup oil
½ to ¾ cup sugar (depending on how sweet you like your hallah)

1¼ cups warm water

2. Combine all the ingredients (including the yeast mixture) and mix well. Cover and set aside to rise for an hour or more in a warm place (or overnight in the refrigerator), until doubled in size.
3. After the first rising, punch the dough down and cut in half. Remove an olive-sized portion to "separate the <u>h</u>allah," and say the *brakhah*:

   בָּרוּךְ אַתָּה יי אֱלֹהֵינוּ מֶלֶךְ הָעוֹלָם אֲשֶׁר קִדְּשָׁנוּ בְּמִצְוֹתָיו וְצִוָּנוּ לְהַפְרִישׁ חַלָּה.

   Barukh *Attah Adonai Eloheinu Melekh ha-Olam asher kidshanu b'mitzvotav v'tzivanu l'hafrish <u>h</u>allah.*

   Blessed are You, Eternal, our God, Ruler of the Cosmos, Who has sanctified us with commandments and commanded us to separate <u>h</u>allah.

   (However, you do not have to make a *brakhah* on separating <u>h</u>allah with only 6 cups of flour, only if the recipe is doubled.)

4. Out of each half, make three strips to braid. After braiding the dough, place on a greased pan to rise again. Make an egg wash (one whole egg and a little water mixed together) to brush over the top of the braided <u>h</u>allah. Sprinkle with poppy seeds or sesame seeds if desired. Allow to rise another 20 minutes in a warm place. Bake in a preheated oven for 45 minutes.

   It is traditional to ritually wash your hands and say a *brakhah*. You can find this *brakhah* on page 129.

   Before you and your students eat the <u>h</u>allah, say this *brakhah*:

   בָּרוּךְ אַתָּה יי אֱלֹהֵינוּ מֶלֶךְ הָעוֹלָם הַמּוֹצִיא לֶחֶם מִן הָאָרֶץ.

   Barukh Attah Adonai Eloheinu Melekh ha-Olam ha-Motzi le<u>h</u>em min ha-aretz.

   Blessed are You, Eternal, our God, Ruler of the Cosmos, Who brings out bread from the earth.

Other Craft Ideas for Creation

Make a mural from a roll of butcher paper depicting each day of creation. This could also be carried out throughout the year with a new picture of the parashah each week to create your own Torah scroll.

Create a picture of each day of the week and bind into a book, either individual books for each child or as a group project to add to your storybook corner.

The Garden of Eden

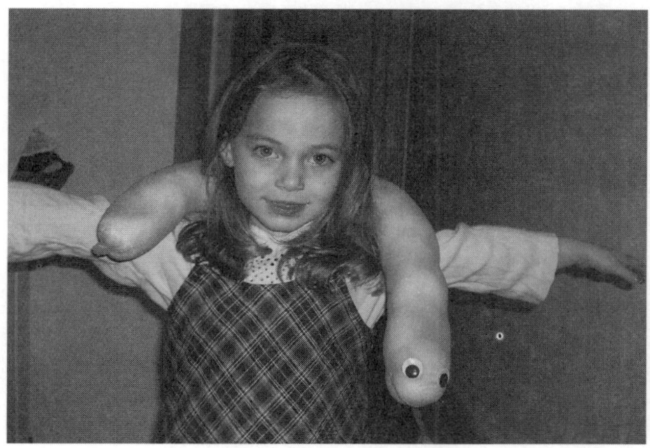

(Prop suggestions: a snake made from the leg of a pantyhose stuffed with poly-fiber fill, with glue on eyes and a tongue, and legs attached with Velcro to be removed at the end of the story; plastic apples; animal puppets. Choose a child to be the Tree of Knowledge to hold the apples, and drape the snake around the child's neck.)

God created the first man and women and named them Adam and Eve (*Hava*). They lived in a beautiful place called the Garden of Eden (*Gan Eden*). The garden was filled with all sorts of plants and flowers and fruit trees.

Walking in the garden there was a snake. In those times snakes had legs like most of the other animals. The snake saw that Adam and Eve were picking the fruit from several of the trees. But they did not pick the fruit from the Tree of Knowledge. One day, as Eve was picking fruit, the snake asked, "Why don't you pick the fruit from the Tree of Knowledge?"

"Because God warned us not to eat from the fruit of that tree," Eve answered.

"Oh, but you don't know what you're missing. The fruit from that tree is the juiciest and also the most delicious fruit in the whole garden." Having said that, the snake reached up and picked a fruit from a branch of the Tree of Knowledge and handed it to Eve. "Here, just try it. You will love this fruit!"

Eve reached to take the fruit but then withdrew her hand quickly. "No, no! I'm not supposed to eat it. God told us not to."

"Oh come on, just one little bite. Try it, you'll like it. Surely nothing could happen if you take just one tiny bite!" replied the snake.

"Well, I guess it would be okay. I'll take a tiny bite," Eve agreed. And she took a small bite. "Oh my, this IS delicious. What kind of fruit is this?" she asked.

"Oh, I don't really know. Maybe it's a fig, or an orange. Maybe it's an apple. But it certainly is delicious, don't you agree?" answered the snake. Eve agreed, and gave some of the fruit to Adam.

When God saw how the snake tricked Eve and Adam, God was quite angry with the snake. God said to the snake, "You have been evil. It was wrong of you to trick this woman into eating the fruit. For this, you will lose your legs and your ability to talk and from now on you will have to slither along on your belly."

And the snake's legs were gone from that time on, and forever more all snakes have had to crawl around on their bellies. And now, Adam and Eve had to leave the beautiful garden and work for their food.

ADDITIONAL MULTIMEDIA IDEAS

COOKING

Make baked apples. Then make soft pretzel snakes to put inside the hole in the apple.

Soft Pretzels (makes 12)

4 cups water
2 tablespoons baking soda
2 tablespoons coarse salt (optional)

1. In a large pot, put 4 cups water, 2 tablespoons baking soda and 2 tablespoons coarse salt (optional).

1 cup warm water
1 package dry active yeast (2¼ teaspoons)
1½ cups bread flour
2 tablespoons vegetable oil
½ teaspoon salt
1¼ cups flour

2. In a bowl, dissolve the yeast in the warm water and let stand for 10 minutes. Add the vegetable oil, salt and 1½ cups flour. Stir together until thoroughly combined. Add remaining flour and knead dough for 5 minutes. Let the dough rest for 1 hour.
3. Divide the dough into 12 equal shapes and form them into small balls. Let them rest for 15 minutes. Roll them out into "snakes" or form them into pretzel shapes. Preheat oven to 475 degrees.

4. After the pretzels have risen for a half hour bring the pot of water and baking soda to a boil. Add the pretzels to the boiling water for 1 minute. Remove and place on a greased sheet pan. Sprinkle with coarse salt and bake for 12 minutes.

BOOKS

The Seventh Day by Deborah Bodin-Cohen

Adam and Eve's First Sunset by Sandy Eisenberg-Sasso

Finding the Fruits of Peace—Cain and Abel by Sandy Eisenberg-Sasso

SONGS

Tune: "Frère Jacques"—traditional, with adaptations by the authors

In the beginning (echo back)
Bereshit (echo back)
God (Hashem) made the whole world (echo)
It was good! (echo back)

God (Hashem) created (echo) night and day (echo)
That was on the first day (echo) It was good! (echo)

God (Hashem) created (echo) Sky and clouds (echo)
That was on the second day (echo) It was good! (echo)

God (Hashem) created (echo) Land and plants (echo)
That was on the third day (echo) It was good! (echo)

God (Hashem) created (echo) Sun, moon, and stars (echo)
That was on the fourth (echo) It was good! (echo)

God (Hashem) created (echo) birds and fish (echo)
That was on the fifth day (echo) It was good! (echo)

God (Hashem) created (echo) Adam and Eve (echo)
That was on the sixth day It was good! (echo)

Then God (Hashem) rested (echo)
M'nuhah (echo)
That was on the seventh day (echo) Tov Me'od! (echo)

(Repeat first four lines)

Israeli traditional

Yom Rishon, avodah
Yom Sheini, avodah
Yom Shlishi, avodah, avodah
Yom R'vi'i, avodah
Yom Hamishi, avodah
Yom Shishi, avodah, avodah
Yom Shabbat, M'nuhah (repeat 3 times)

"Of Course It Was Hashem" by Uncle Moishe, Volume 3

1, 2, 3, 4, 5, 6 days Hashem works in such wonderful ways!

Chorus:
Who made the sky so blue? Not you!
Who made the great big sea? Not me!
Who made the heavens and the earth? Not them!
Of course it was Hashem! It was Hashem!

On the first day He made the dark and the light.
On the second day He made the big blue sky.

(chorus)

On the third day He made the grass on the ground,
the leaves and the trees we see all around.

On the fourth day He made the sun so bright,
the moon and the stars that shine through the night.

(chorus)

On the fifth day He made the birds and the fish,
Animals and man were made on the sixth.

The seventh day a gift to His people He gave,
to rest and rejoice in the things that He made.

Parashat Bereshit Family Discussion

(from *Morah, Morah, Teach Me Torah*)

This is the first parashah (portion) in the first book (of five books) of the Torah. The word Bereshit means "in the beginning." This parashah is about the creation of the world.

On day one God made a separation between the light and the dark (day and night). On day two, a space between the waters was made ,and the top was called the sky. On day three, the waters were gathered and the land was formed; then plants and trees were created. On day four, the lights in the sky were created (sun in the day and moon and stars at night). On day five, the fish in the seas and birds in the sky were created. On day six, God made people (Adam and Eve) and all the animals. On the seventh day, God rested (*m'nuhah*) from God's work (*avodah*). God saw that all that was created was good.

God created the Garden of Eden (*Gan Eden*) for Adam and Eve to live in. They could eat any fruit in the garden except from the tree in the center of the garden (the Tree of Knowledge). But a snake tricked Eve into eating the fruit, and she got Adam to eat too. So as punishment, the snake lost its ability to talk and it could no longer walk on legs. Adam and Eve had to leave the garden and work for their food from then on.

Family Discussion Questions:

1. (Q) How many days did it take God to create the world? (A) Six. On the seventh day God rested.
2. (Q) What were the names of the first two people? (A) Adam and Eve.
3. (Q) Where did they live? (A) *Gan Eden*—the Garden of Eden.

NOAH

Last week we learned how the world was created. Many years later there lived a man named Noah (*Noah* in Hebrew). He was a farmer, and he had a wife and three sons. Each son also had a wife. Noah was a good man. He worked hard on his farm and supplied food for his family. He always did what God wanted him to do.

One day God spoke to Noah: "Noah, there are many people in this world who are wicked. They do selfish and unkind things to other people. I am very angry with them, and I am going to punish them. I'm going to send a great rain that will cover all the earth. But because you and your family are good people, I will save you. I want you to be safe when the flood comes. This is what you must do. You must build a large boat, an ark. You must build it with the wood I tell you and make it the size that I instruct you, 50 cubits wide, 300 cubits long ,and 30 cubits high. Then you will take two of every animal large and small, but seven pairs of kosher animals, and put them on the ark. Bring enough food for all to eat too."

So Noah started to work. He cut down the trees and took the wood that God told him to use, and he made a frame for the boat and put tar on the inside and outside so the boat would not sink. It took Noah 120 years to finish the ark! Whenever someone walked by Noah as he worked, they would ask what he was doing. Noah explained that God was unhappy with the way people were behaving. They were not behaving kindly. God gave the people a lot of time to do *t'shuvah* (say "I'm sorry") and to change their unkind ways, 120 years!

Noah was instructed to bring seven pairs of kosher animals and two of every other kind of animal on the earth and put them in the boat, along with his wife, and his sons and their wives. As soon as they were on the ark, the rain began. It rained for forty days and forty nights. The water covered everything on the earth.

One day the rain stopped. The ark landed on Mount Ararat. Noah sent a dove out to see if the land was dry. When the dove came back with a leaf and twig from an olive tree (one of the seven species from Israel), then Noah knew that the land was dry. When Noah looked up into the sky, he saw a rainbow (*keshet* in Hebrew). Noah built an altar and thanked God for keeping them safe. God promised never again to cause a flood to cover the earth. Every time we see a rainbow we are reminded to be kind and we are reminded of God's promise.

SONGS

Tune: "Johnny Works with One Hammer" (traditional)

Noah worked with one hammer, one hammer, one hammer
Noah worked with one hammer, to build himself an ark.
Noah worked with one saw, one saw, one saw
Noah worked with one saw, to build himself an ark.
When the ark was finished, finished, finished
When the ark was finished, he brought the animals
The animals came in pairs, in pairs, in pairs
The animals came in pairs, so they could all be safe.
The rain came pouring down, down, down
The rain came pouring down, and then there was a flood.
When the rain had stopped, stopped, stopped
When the rain had stopped, a rainbow did appear.
The rainbow was a promise, a promise, a promise
The rainbow was a promise God will care for you.

"Rise and Shine" (traditional folk song)

Chorus: Rise and shine and give God your glory, glory.
Rise and shine and give God your glory, glory.
Rise and shine and (clap) give God your glory, glory,
Children of the Lord.

God told Noah there's gonna be a floody, floody
God told Noah there's gonna be a floody, floody,
Get those animals (clap) out of the muddy, muddy
Children of the Lord.

(Chorus)

God told Noah to build him an arky, arky
God told Noah to build him an arky, arky
Make it out of (clap) hickory barky, barky
Children of the Lord.

(Chorus)

The animals, they came on, they came on by twosies
The animals, they came on, they came on by twosies, twosies.
Elephants and (clap) kangaroosies, roosies
Children of the Lord.

(Chorus)

It rained, and poured for forty daysies, daysies
Rained and poured for forty daysies,
drove those animals (clap) almost crazy, crazy
Children of the Lord.

(Chorus)

The sun came out and dried up the landy, landy
Sun came out and dried up the landy, landy.
Everything was (clap) fine and dandy, dandy
Children of the Lord.

Tune: "Twinkle, Twinkle Little Star" (traditional)

There were bad people in the land, but Noah was a righteous man.
He always tried to do what's right, he loved God with all his might.
So God told Noah what to do, gather animals two by two.
Build an ark, a very big boat, cover with pitch so it will float.

Make it big and make it wide, so all the animals fit inside.
Gather your family, warn your friends, the rains will come, this is the end!
Then the rain began to pour. Hurry up and close the door!
It rained for 40 nights and days, for 150 it floated on the waves.

The ark landed on Ararat Mount, 40 more days did Noah count.
Then a dove was sent to see if all was safe for his family.
The dove returned with a branch from a tree, so they built an altar for all to see.
Noah thanked God and what do you know, God sent Noah a beautiful rainbow.

Noah was a righteous man, "Be fruitful and multiply—fill the land!"

MULTIMEDIA IDEAS

"ASK ME" STICKER: Ask me what Noah built.

SCIENCE: 1) Practice floating and sinking experiments. Create a boat out of wood to see if it will float. Add small plastic animals to the water table to put on your boat.

2) Try some water absorption experiments. Test various objects to see which ones will absorb water using eydroppers. Drop water on such items as a rubber glove, tissue, sponge, rock, sock, etc.

CRAFT: 1) Create a mural of Noah's ark with the animals and with a rainbow over it.

2) Make animal masks to act out the story of Noah's ark.

COOKING: Bake animal cookies. To make a boat, bake a cake in a round Pyrex bowl sprayed well with cooking oil spray. Dump out the cake onto a tray, spread cake icing on the cake, and stick animal crackers on the outside. Then eat!

MATH: 1) Look at and collect things that come in pairs.

2) Discuss how you could make a blueprint to build an ark. Have the children make plans to build it, finding the materials for building. This is a good time to talk about measurements in building a structure, because God was very specific about how the ark should be built.

Parashat Noah Family Discussion

(from *Morah, Morah, Teach Me Torah*)

This week's parashah is all about Noah (*Noah*) and the flood. Noah was a righteous man in his time. He and his wife and three sons were farmers. The people of that time were not kind and did not follow God's laws. God told Noah that there would be a big flood that would swallow up the earth, but that Noah and his family would be safe. God told Noah to build an ark and to take seven pairs of kosher animals and two of every other kind of animal onto the ark. It took Noah 120 years to build the ark, plenty of time for the people to repent and change their ways!

When Noah finished his work and brought his wife, family, and the animals onto the ark, it began to rain. It rained for 40 days and 40 nights! For 150 days the ark floated on the waves. Finally, the ark landed on Mount Ararat. Noah sent a dove to see if the land was dry. The dove returned with a leaf from an olive tree (one of the seven species of Israel). God sent a rainbow (*keshet*) as a promise that there would never again be a flood on the earth like that. Noah saw that it would be safe to exit the ark and start life over again. He built an altar to say thank you to God for saving his family.

Family Discussion Questions:

1. (Q) Why did God send a flood? (A) Because people were not being kind and listening to God.
2. (Q) Why did God choose Noah? (A) Because he was a righteous man and did the right thing.
3. (Q) How many animals did he take with him? (A) Seven pairs of kosher animals and two of every other kind of animal.
4. (Q) How long did it rain? (A) Forty days and nights.
5. (Q) What did God send as a promise to never flood the earth again? (A) A rainbow (*keshet*).

LEKH-LEKHA

In our last parashah we learned about Noah. Noah had children, and his children had children, and one of those children was named Terah. Terah had a son named Avram (Abram). Avram was the first Jewish person! According to midrash, at the age of three, Avram figured out that there is one God who rules the whole world. This is a great parashah to act out with your children.

In the parashah Lekh-Lekha, which means "GO (YOU GO)!" God tells Avram, "Go from your land, from your father's house to a land that I will show you." How would you feel if someone asked you to leave your home and you didn't even know where you were going? Pretty scary! But Avram had complete faith and trust in God, so he started packing. He gathered his wife, Sarai, and his nephew Lot, all their belongings, and all their flocks and started out on a long journey. They were leaving Haran and traveling to Canaan (Israel), and they stopped for the night and set up their tents.

Have the children hold the ends of a parachute and pull it over their heads and under them to make a tent. As you act out the traveling, have the children walk, holding the ends of the parachute, which will be the tent, and chant:

> "Oh, we walk and we walk and we walk and we walk, and we walk and we walk and we walk, then we stop."
>
> They were tired so they put up their tent, and the tent went up, up, up, up, up [everyone raise the parachute up].
>
> Then down, down, down, down, down.
>
> Then we walked and we walked, etc.

You can do this a few times to show how far they walked to get to their new place.

SONG **(tune: "We're Going to Kentucky, We're Going to the Fair"—traditional; lyrics by Martha Resnick and Diane Holsten, with adaptations by the authors)**

We're going to Canaan
We're leaving from Haran
To a place God will show us
With Sarah and Avraham
We're packing up our things
We're traveling very far
It's taking us a long, long time
Oy, I wish we had a car!

The shepherds who took care of Avram and Lot's flocks were not being kind to each other. So Avram said, "Families should not fight! We should separate; choose where you would like to live. If you go north, I'll go south. If you go south, I'll go north."

Lot was very selfish, he cared only about himself. Lot saw that in one direction there was a beautiful stream, and lots of grass and trees, so he chose that way, toward Sodom. Avram was very kind to Lot.

God saw how kind Avram was and blessed him. God changed Avram's name to Abraham (Avraham) and changed Sarai's name to Sarah. Then God blessed Abraham and said, "I will make you the father of a multitude of nations. You will have as many children as there are grains of sand on the beach, and as many children as there are stars in the sky." Now this was pretty interesting because Abraham and Sarah had no children at all! What do you think happens in next week's parashah?

MULTIMEDIA IDEAS

"ASK ME" STICKER: Ask me who would have as many children as stars in the sky. (Avraham!)

STORIES: *A Little Boy Named Avram* by Dina Rosenfeld. This story is based on the midrash. A fun story to act out too!

CRAFT: If you read the book *A Little Boy Named Avram* by Dina Rosenfeld, you can create puppets based on the story. Using craft foam, cut out a sun and glue it to a craft stick, and cut out a moon and glue it to a craft stick. Make a puppet of Avram and act out the story.

COOKING: Make star-shaped cookies and top them with "sand" sugar ("as many children as stars in the sky and as many children as grains of sand on the beach"). See recipe for sugar cookies in Bereshit (page 13).

DRAMA: Bring in a small tent, or make one with a parachute or sheet, and act out the story.

MATH: Draw a suitcase on paper and have the kids draw or cut out from magazines ten things they would take with them on their trip. Ask them to count the items in English and Hebrew!

Avram and the Idols (based on midrash)

Avram's father, Terah, didn't believe that there was one God. He built idols (statues) that represented gods for all kinds of different things. There was a god of rain, a god of growing things, a god of fire, and one who took care of the earth. But Jewish people don't pray to many gods; we pray to just one, God. That's what Avram believed.

Terah had a store where he sold idols to people. One day when Avram was in his father's store, he asked his father, "Does the god of the moon really take care of the moon? Does he care about me? What do the gods look like? Do they each look different?"

"Why, yes, each god looks different, just as people look different," answered Terah.

"How do you know what the gods look like? Have you ever seen them?" asked Avram.

"No, I've never seen them. Nobody has, but I just know that they look like people. Now go outside and do your chores and stop asking so many questions. You are making the gods angry," said Terah.

Avram went outside, but he didn't stop asking questions. One day he was alone with all the idols in his father's store. There were large ones, ugly ones, fat ones, and short ones. He started dusting them and arranging all the idols on the shelves. He talked to them but knew they couldn't hear him or answer him. A lady came into the story to buy an idol. As payment she brought a big, beautiful bowl of fruit. Avram sold the lady an idol, but he didn't think it was the right thing to do. He became angry with himself and started smashing all the idols with a hammer. He took the hammer and put it in the hands of the biggest idol, with the fruit bowl in front of the idol. Just then, his father, Terah, came back to the store and saw what Avram had done, and he exclaimed, "What happened in here?"

Avram answered, "A lady brought some fruit to buy an idol. All the idols started arguing over who would get to keep the fruit, and they started fighting and the biggest idol won the fight."

"Don't tell me such stories, don't you know that idols are made of stone? They can't move or hear, or feel or see!"

"You're right! They are made of stone, so why do you pray to them?" replied Avram. And that is when Avram taught his own father that there is only one God!

RELATED SONGS

1) SONG/PRAYER: The Shema

Shema Yisrael Adonai Eloheinu Adonai Eḫad.
Hear, Israel (Jewish people), the Eternal is our God, the Eternal is One.

2) SONG "Hashem Is Here" by Uncle Moishe, Volume 1

Hashem is here, Hashem is there, Hashem is truly everywhere.
Hashem is here, Hashem is there, Hashem is truly everywhere.
Up, up, down, down, right, left and all around,
here, there and everywhere, that's where He can be found.

3) SONG (Tune: "There Were Three Jolly Fisherman"—traditional, with adaptations by the authors)

The first Jew's name was Avraham (2x)
Avra, Avra, ham, ham, ham (2x)
The first Jew's name was Avraham.
He believed there's one God. (2x)
Avra, Avra, ham, ham, ham (2x)
He believed there's one God.
He always welcomed guests to his tent. (2x)
Avra, Avra, ham, ham, ham (2x)
He always welcomed guests to his tent.
His wife's name was Sarah (2x)
Avra, Avra, ham, ham, ham (2x)
His wife's name was Sarah.

4) SONG (tune: "Mary Wore Her Red Dress"—traditional)

God told Avraham, Avraham, Avraham,
God told Avraham, it's time to leave your home.
It's time to leave your homeland, homeland, homeland,
It's time to leave your homeland, I'll show you where to go.
You'll have as many children, children, children,
You'll have as many children, as stars in the sky.
You'll be a great nation, nation, nation,
You'll be a great nation, *lekh-lekha.*

5) CHANTING GAME

Lekh-lekha, lekh-lekha
Where are we going?
Lekh-lekha, lekh-lekha
God will show you where.
Lekh-lekha, lekh-lekha
How will we get there?
Lekh-lekha, lekh-lekha
God will show you how.
Lekh-lekha, lekh-lekha
We must *(jump, hop, march, crawl, let kids pick, etc.)* to get there
Lekh-lekha, lekh-lekha
God will show you where.

(repeat with various movements)

6) SONG (tune: "Home On The Range"—lyrics by Lisa Ginsburg-Arber, with adaptations by the authors)

Home, home in my tent
Where many hours with Sarah are spent.
All day I tend sheep
Then I come home and sleep
And I'm happy to be in my tent.

Now Canaan is my home
I know I'm with God, not alone.
God gave us this land
So come take my hand [hold your neighbor's hand]
And we'll make a new life in Canaan.

Parashat Lekh Lekha Family Discussion

(from *Morah, Morah, Teach Me Torah*)

This week's parashah is Lekh-Lekha, which means "You go!" In this parashah, we introduce Avram (who later becomes Avraham, the father of the Jewish people). Avram is married to Sarai (who becomes Sarah), and they live in Haran. God tells Avram to go from his home-land, from his father's house to a place that God will show him. What faith and trust Avram has!

So they pack up all their belongings and together with Avram's nephew Lot, they set off on their journey. They travel a long, long time, and as they travel, Lot's shepherds and Avram's shepherds begin to argue. Avram says, "Families should not fight! Choose where you want to go. If you go north, I'll go south. If you go south, I'll go north." Lot was selfish, so he chose to go where there was a beautiful stream and lots of fresh grass for his flocks, near Sodom.

God saw how kind Avram was and blessed him. Avram's name was changed to Avraham and Sarai's name was changed to Sarah. God told them, "I will bless you and make you a great nation with as many children as stars in the sky." This is pretty interesting, as they are very old and have NO children!

Family Discussion Questions:

1. (Q) What does *lekh-lekha* mean? (A) You go!
2. (Q) What happened when Lot's shepherds and Avram's shepherds began to fight? (A) Avram let Lot choose where he wanted to live.
3. (Q) What was the blessing that God gave to Avram and Sarai? (A) God changed their names and blessed them as a great nation with as many children as stars in the sky.
4. (Q) What does it mean that Avraham and Sarah would have as many children as stars in the sky? (A) Their family in the future would be very large.

VA-YERA

We love to incorporate drama into our *Kabbalat Shabbat* program. This parashah is a fun story to act out! It's also a story about *hakhnasat or<u>h</u>im*, the mitzvah of inviting guests. So invite some guests to your classroom today!

Remember in last week's parashah, God told Avraham that he would have as many children as stars in the sky?

In this week's parashah, Va-Yera, Avraham receives three visitors. *Va-yera* means "And God appears". Who do you think the three visitors will be?

Avraham loves to have guests visit him. His tent has four doors so he can receive guests from all directions! Avraham is very excited; he runs to greet the strangers and invites them into his tent. He asks Sarah to make some bread while he prepares some meat. As the food is cooking, Avraham gives his guests some fruit and water, and he even washes their feet! The three men who come to visit are actually messengers from God. Sarah is bringing in the food when the messengers tell Avraham that in one year Sarah will have a baby boy. Sarah starts to laugh! She chuckles to herself, "Me? I'm an old woman already. I can't have a baby!" But, in one year Sarah does have a beautiful baby boy, and they name him Yitz<u>h</u>ak (Isaac). The name Yitz<u>h</u>ak means "laughter"!

SONG (tune: "Mary Wore Her Red Dress"—traditional)

Three guests are coming to visit us, visit us, visit us.
Three guests are coming to visit us.
We welcome you today.
Come and have some bread with us, bread with us, bread with us.
Come and have some bread with us.
We welcome you today.
Sarah had a baby boy, baby boy, baby boy.
Sarah had a baby boy.
We welcome you today.
The baby's name was Yitzhak, Yitzhak, Yitzhak.
The baby's name was Yitzhak.
We welcome you today.
Yitzhak means laughter, laughter, laughter.
Yitzhak means laughter.
We welcome you today.

SONG (tune: "Home on the Range"—Traditional; Lyrics by Lisa Ginsburg-Arber, with adaptations by the authors)

Home, home in my tent
Where many hours with Sarah are spent.
All day I tend sheep
Then I come home and sleep
And I'm happy to be in my tent.

Now Canaan is my home
I know I'm with God, not alone.
God gave us this land
So come take my hand [hold your neighbor's hand]
And we'll make a new life in Canaan

Three guests are coming I see
To visit Sarah and me.
We'll wash their feet, give them something to eat
They have news for our family.

"A baby you will have."
That made Sarah laugh.
"I am so old, a baby I'm told
Baby Yitzhak, we are so glad!"

MULTIMEDIA IDEAS

"ASK ME" STICKER: Ask me what Sarah did when she was told she was going to have a baby.

STORY/MATH: *The Doorbell Rang* by Pat Hutchins. It's a story about friends who come over and share cookies.

STORY: *Dovy and the Surprise Guest* by Goldie Golding.

CRAFT: Make a tent out of poster board and decorate it. Make it with four doors like Avraham's tent, and use the little people and toy animals to play with it.

COOKING: Make pita bread and hummus to share with guests you invite. You can always share with another class in your school or a neighbor.

Pita Bread

1 cup warm water	1½ teaspoon yeast	½ teaspoon salt
1 tablespoon sugar	3 cups flour	1 tablespoon oil

1. Combine the water, sugar, and yeast in a mixing bowl and let stand for 5 minutes, until foamy.
2. Add salt and flour, 1 cup at a time, and incorporate it with the dough hook or by hand. Knead and add more flour if the dough is too sticky.
3. Lightly oil a large bowl or spray with cooking spray. Put the dough in the bowl, and turn it to coat with oil. Cover with a towel and let rise in a warm place for about an hour, until doubled (or in the refrigerator overnight).
4. Punch down the dough and transfer to a heavily floured surface. Knead for 5 minutes. Divide into 6-12 equal pieces.
5. Knead each piece of dough for a few minutes, then roll out into a very thin circle. Let each pita rest for 30 minutes.
6. Preheat oven to 500 degrees. Place a cookie sheet in the oven for a minute or two, until warm.
7. Brush the cookie sheet with oil (or spray with cooking spray). Arrange the pita bread so that they are not touching.

For soft pita bread: Bake until puffy and light brown, about 6–8 minutes. Wrap the pitas together in a towel, place in a paper bag, close it up, and let sit for 15 minutes.

For crispy pita bread: Bake 10-12 minutes, and let cool on a rack.

Hummus

2 cups canned chickpeas, liquid reserved
⅔ cup tahina paste
5 tablespoons olive oil, divided
¼ cup lemon juice
3 cloves garlic
Salt and pepper to taste
1 teaspoon paprika
1 tablespoon fresh parsley, chopped (optional)

1. In a food processor, puree the chickpeas, tahina, 3 tablespoons olive oil, lemon juice, and garlic until smooth, adding a little of the reserved liquid if the mixture seems too thick. Season with salt and pepper.
2. Transfer to a shallow bowl or plate. Combine the paprika and the remaining 2 tablespoons olive oil (optional), drizzle the mixture over the top, and garnish with chopped parsley, if desired. Serve with pita bread triangles. Makes about 3 cups.

"Sodom and Gemorrah"

Remember when Avraham, Sarah, and Lot moved to Canaan and Avraham let Lot choose which direction he wanted to live? Well, Lot chose to move to Sodom near a beautiful stream.

The towns of Sodom and Gemorrah were very near each other and the people in those towns were not very kind. They did whatever they wanted, whenever they wanted. The town was a mess! God could see that only bad people lived there and wanted to destroy the two towns. He told Avraham about the plan.

Avraham said, "Wait, what if there are fifty good people who live there? Will you kill the fifty good people along with the others?"

God said, "Okay, I'll save the towns if there are fifty good people."

Then Avraham asked, "What if there are only forty good people? Will you still destroy the towns?"

And God said, "Okay, if there are forty good people, I will spare the towns." (Repeat scenario decreasing by ten until you get to ten people).

Now, Avraham tried arguing with God one more time. "What if there are only ten good people?"

So, God agreed that if there were ten good people God would save the towns. But there weren't ten good people in all of Sodom and Gemorrah!

So Avraham asked God one more question: "Please, my nephew Lot lives in Sodom. Please, could you spare his life and the lives of his family?"

God agreed. Lot and his family were told to pack their things and leave Sodom and NOT TO LOOK BACK! And if God tells you to do something, you better listen! But Lot's wife couldn't help herself; she looked back and was turned into a pillar of salt—Like a statue. Oy!

MULTIMEDIA IDEAS

MOVEMENT: Play freeze tag or freeze dance to music and act like a statue when the leader says "freeze!"

SCIENCE: Make salt crystals. Put lots of coarse kosher salt in a bowl of water and let it evaporate (it takes a few days). Look for the salt crystals.

CRAFT: Show pictures of salt formations and different kinds of pillars. Talk about what a pillar of salt might look like. Talk about what people who were turned into salt would look like. Using glue and coarse kosher salt, try to make some salt formations.

Parashat Va-Yera Family Discussion

(from *Morah, Morah, Teach Me Torah*)

Va-yera means "God appeared." This week Avraham and Sarah receive three guests in their tent. This is the mitzvah of *hakhnasat orhim*—inviting guests. Avraham is known as a wonderful host. As he sees three men out in the distance, he runs out to greet them. He invites them to his tent, offers them food and drinks, and even washes their feet! (Such service!) The men are actually messengers from God, and they tell Avraham that Sarah will have a baby in a year. Sarah laughs (she is almost ninety years old!), but in a year, she does have a baby and they name him Yitzhak (Isaac), which means "laughter."

In this week's parashah another story occurs. Remember that Lot moved to Sodom? In Sodom and Gemorrah (a town nearby) the people were not being kind. They were very mean, and God wanted to destroy them all. Avraham argues with God saying, "But what if there are fifty righteous people there? Will you still destroy everyone?" God agrees not to destroy the towns. Avraham argues down to ten righteous people. But there were not even ten, so Avraham asks God to save Lot and his family before the town is destroyed. God warns them NOT to look back as they leave the town. Lot's wife can't help it; she peeks and is turned into a pillar of salt.

Family Discussion Questions:

1. (Q) Who are the guests who visit Sarah and Avraham? (A) Messengers from God.
2. (Q) How we can make guests in our home feel welcome?
3. (Q) What is the baby's name and what does it mean? (A) Yitzhak, "laughter."
4. (Q) What happens to Lot's wife? (A) She looks back at Sodom burning and she is turned into a pillar of salt—like a statue.

<u>H</u>AYYEI SARAH

In last week's parashah three guests visited Avraham and Sarah and told them that they would have a baby. They did have a baby, and his name was Yitz<u>h</u>ak. Yitz<u>h</u>ak means "laughter."

This week's parashah is called <u>H</u>ayyei Sarah, which means "the life of Sarah." Sarah's son Yitz<u>h</u>ak grew up. His father, Avraham, was now very old, and he realized that it was time for him to find a wife for Yitz<u>h</u>ak.

"I'm an old man, now. Before I die I must go and find a wife for my Yitz<u>h</u>ak and bring her here. I will choose a wife from our people, not from the people living in Canaan who worship idols," thought Avraham.

So he called for his trusted servant Eliezer and said, "I want you to find a wife for my son, Yitz<u>h</u>ak. Go to <u>H</u>aran, the land of my family, and choose a wife. Then bring her back here to me."

The next day, Eliezer rounded up ten camels, gathered gifts of gold and silver, and started on his journey. Camels are like a desert ship; they can last many days traveling in the desert without water. But then, when they drink, they drink A LOT!

(Act out this song, making lines of children, who will be the camels. As you say the word "humps," the children do a wave dip, bending their knees and standing up to signify the hump.)

SONG: "Saul the Gamal"—(tune: *Sally the Camel,* lyrics by Irene Light)
Saul the gamal had 5 humps (3x)
So ride, Sauly, ride, boom, boom, boom, boom! *(wiggle your tush on the booms)*
Saul the gamal had 4 humps (3x)
So ride, Sauly, ride, boom, boom, boom, boom!
Saul the gamal had 3 humps (3x)
So ride, Sauly, ride, boom, boom, boom, boom!
Saul the gamal had 2 humps (3x)

So ride, Sauly, ride, boom, boom, boom, boom!
Saul the gamal had 1 hump (3x)
So ride, Sauly, ride, boom, boom, boom, boom!
Saul the gamal had no humps (3x)
'cause Sauly was a horse, of course!

After traveling for many days, Eliezer came to a city. Near the gates to the city was a well. Traveling all that way made him very thirsty so he went to the well to get a drink. There were many young women standing near the well.

"This might be a place where I might find a wife for Yitzhak, but how will I know which one will be the right one for him? God, please give me a sign to show me which one to choose. The right girl will offer water to the camels as well."

He could tell that the camels were thirsty, too, so Eliezer went over to the well to get water. In those days, you couldn't get water from a faucet; you got water from a well deep in the ground. Beside the well was a beautiful young lady filling up jars with water. She smiled at him and came over to him.

"Please, I would like very much to have a drink of water," Eliezer said.

At first she didn't say anything. Then she said to him, "You have traveled a long way. Here, have a drink of water from the well. And I'll give your camels some water, too." This was the sign that he was looking for. Now he knew that she was very kind and that she was the right girl for Yitzhak.

Midrash (Rabbinic story) says that as she drew water from the well, the water rose up to meet her because of her kindness (hesed).

"You are very kind. What is your name?" asked Eliezer. "I am Rivka [Rebecca], the daughter of Betuel," she answered.

SONG (tune: "He Waded in the Water and He Got His Ankles Wet"—traditional; lyrics by Diane Holsten with adaptations by the authors)

Eliezer had ten camels, they were thirsty at the well (3x)
And Rivka gave them all a drink
Rivka gave them all some water (3x)
Because she was so kind

SONG (tune: "U'she'avtim Mayim"—Israeli folk song)

Of course you should dance to this song as well!

Eliezer went to find
A special wife for Yitzhak.
Who will be the right girl?
Someone who is very kind.

Chorus:

Mayim, mayim, mayim, mayim
Hey! *Mayim* at the well. (2x)
Hey, hey, hey, hey
Mayim (6x)
At the well.
Mayim (6x)
At the well.

Or in English:

Water, water, water, water
Hey! Water at the well. (2x)
Hey, hey, hey, hey
Water (6x)
At the well.
Water (6x)
At the well.

Eliezer asked a girl
for a drink from the well.
"Yes, of course, you may drink
And water for your camels as well."

(Chorus)

Rivka was this girl's name,
She was sweet and she was kind.
Yitzhak fell in love with her,
A better wife you couldn't find.

(Chorus)

Eliezer said, "Rivka, you are so kind. I want to give you these gifts of gold and silver and these bracelets."

"Oh, that is very kind of you. I will ask my father if you may rest at his house," she said.

"Yes, this woman would be a perfect match to marry Yitzhak. She is thoughtful, kind, and beautiful. I will ask Betuel if I can take Rivka home with me to marry Yitzhak," thought Eliezar to himself.

Rivka wanted to go, and Betuel agreed, so Rivka and Eliezer started on their long journey back to Avraham's country.

When they came to Avraham's house, Yitzhak was waiting and ran over to them. When he heard how kind she was and saw how beautiful Rivka was, he fell in love with her right away and asked for her to be his wife.

MULTIMEDIA ACTIVITIES

"ASK ME" STICKER: Ask me why Rivka was so special. (Because she was so kind.)

LANGUAGE: Act out the story, having the wedding of Yitzhak and Rivka, complete with *huppah*, of course! (Sing *Siman Tov u'Mazel Tov*!)

MATH: Since Rivka carried buckets of water for the camels, have children go outside and fill up buckets of water and carry them for a distance. See how heavy they are. Measure the amounts of water and how many trips it will take to empty the well. Take out the water table and do some water experiments.

SCIENCE: It's a good time to learn about camels and find out what kind of camels live in Israel.

You can also create a volcano to show water rising (as the midrash describes) to meet Rivka. In a disposable pan, mold clay around a yogurt container to create a well (or build a sugar cube well around a yogurt container). In the container, put baking soda and *slowly* pour white vinegar dyed with blue food coloring into the container. And watch what happens!

CRAFT: Make a centerpiece depicting a camel and a desert scene. Put glue on the bottom of a piece of paper or box top, and sprinkle on some sand. Add a camel or two, either a toy one or one made out of clay. Add a well constructed with sugar cubes and glue.

CONSTRUCTION: 1) Build a well out of blocks.

2) Build a well out of modeling clay, and add real stones to the outside. Can you build them on your floor map of Israel?

BOOK: *Kind Little Rivka* by Dina Rosenfeld.

SCIENCE: Put sand into a water table or large baking tray. Add camels and small people, too. Toy camels are available at www.tapirback.com.

SONG: "Camel Caravan" by Carol Boyd Leon, from her CD *Gan Shirim*

Ride a camel, across the land, head up high and, feet in the sand
Sit on top of the humpty-hump, moving forward bumpty-bump.

[Bend your knees on the bumpty-bump]

Parashat Hayyei Sarah Family Discussion

(from *Morah, Morah, Teach Me Torah*)

Hayyei Sarah means "the life of Sarah." Avraham realizes he is getting old and must find a wife for his son, Yitzhak. So Avraham sends his trusted servant Eliezer to Haran to find a wife. Eliezer packs up ten camels and lots of gifts and sets off for Haran. He isn't sure how to find a wife for Yitzhak, so he asks God for help. If Eliezer asks a girl for water and the girl offers water for his camels too, then he will know it is the right girl for Yitzhak. She must be kind!

Soon Eliezer comes to a well and asks a beautiful girl for water. And she offers water for his camels too! It's *bashert* (meant to be)! The girl tells Eliezer her name, Rivka (Rebecca), and offers to bring him home to her father's tent to sleep. Eliezer tells Betuel (her father) all that happened, and all agree that she will return to Canaan with Eliezer to marry Yitzhak.

Family Discussion Questions:

1. (Q) Why does Avraham send Eliezer to Haran? (A) to find a wife for Yitzhak.
2. (Q) How will Eliezer know who is the right girl? (A) She will be very kind—and get water for all his camels.
3. (Q) Does Rikva agree to go to Canaan? (A) Of course!
4. (Q) What are some ways you can be kind like Rivka?

TOLDOT

In last week's parashah, Yitzhak grew up, and it was time for him to get married. Remember when Avraham's servant, Eliezer, went to find Yitzhak a wife and found Rivka (Rebecca) at the well? Yitzhak loved Rivka, and they got married.

This week we read Parashat Toldot—the story of Yitzhak. *Toldot* means "offspring," and "generations"; we learn about the offspring of Yitzhak. Yitzhak and Rivka built a home in Canaan and were blessed with a good life. But one day Rivka came to Yitzhak and said, "We've been blessed with many good things, yet I am unhappy. There is one thing we don't have. We don't have any children. Who will take care of our land when we get old? Who will take care of our animals?"

Yitzhak was sad too. And he said, "Maybe it would help if we prayed to God." So they did.

Many weeks and months passed, and Rivka said to Yitzhak, "I feel something moving inside my belly! I think we are going to have a baby! Now we will be very happy."

As the months passed, Rivka's tummy grew bigger and bigger, and there was a lot of movement inside. She was scared, so she prayed to God for help. God said, "Don't be afraid. You are not going to have just one baby, you will have twin sons. Both sons will become leaders, but in different ways. The first son will be big and strong, but the younger will rule the older one, and I will bless them both."

A few months later, Rivka had twin boys. The first baby was born with lots of red hair. His name was Esav (Esau). When the second baby was born, he was holding onto the heel of his brother. He was smaller than Esav and had smooth skin. The second baby's name was Ya'akov (Jacob). In Hebrew Ya'akov means "on the heel of." Even though they were twins, they looked very different. Twins don't have to look alike; they are often different in many different ways. Do you know any twins?

Years passed and the boys became men. They liked to do different things. Ya'akov liked to stay home and study and cook. And Esav liked to hunt.

Now in those days, the firstborn boy would take over the father's land when the father got too old. It was called his birthright. In some families the older children helped to take care of the younger ones. They had more responsibilities. Esav, who was the oldest, didn't want the responsibility of taking care of the house and land; he just wanted to hunt.

(If you want to act out this story, you could use a toy bow and arrow and faux fur to wrap around Esav's arms and to make a beard. Use sunglasses for the "blind" Yitzhak. Have pots and dishes set out for the stew for Ya'akov.)

One day Esav came home from hunting. He was tired and sweaty and really hungry. When he came into the tent he said, "Something smells so delicious. I'm so hungry, Ya'akov. Give me some of that stew you've made."

Ya'akov was tired as well. He thought for a moment, and then he said, "I'll gladly give you some of this stew, but in exchange for this stew I want you to sell me your birthright. You don't care about keeping the home. You just want to hunt."

Esav was so hungry. He couldn't stand it any longer. "Just take it. I don't care about the birthright!"

He took the stew and ate it as fast as he could. Should he have done that? Remember what God told Rivka when she was pregnant, that the younger son would rule the older one?

In time, Yitzhak grew old, and his eyes grew weaker until he couldn't see any more.

Yitzhak said, "Esav, I'm getting old and I can't take care of this house anymore. It's your job now. First, go hunt for my favorite meat and prepare it for me. Then I will bless you and you will be the head of the family."

"Thank you, I'll go now." Esav took his bow and arrow and left Yitzhak's tent.

Rivka overheard the conversation and went to Ya'akov and said, "Esav is hunting for food for your father, and then he will bless him and make him the head of the family. I know that you are the one who should be blessed as the firstborn, so do as I say! Prepare two young goats, and I will cook them the way your father likes. Then you will pretend to be Esav and take the food to your blind father. He will bless you, instead."

Ya'akov said, "But Mother, I can't fool my father. Esav is a hairy man, and my skin is smooth. If father touches me, he will know that I am Ya'akov and will be angry with me for trying to trick him."

Rivka replied, "Do as I say. Wrap the goat skins around your arms, and when your father touches you, he will think you are your brother."

So Ya'akov did as he was told and said, "Father, I am here with the food you asked for. Eat and I will be blessed."

"Which son are you?" The blind Yitzhak asked.

"I am Esav. Please sit and eat so you can give me your blessing."

Yitzhak asked, "How did you come back so quickly, my son?"

Ya'akov replied, "God helped me."

"Come closer so that I may touch you," Yitzchak said.

When Ya'akov, pretending to be Esav, came closer, Yitzhak touched him and felt his hairy arms. "The voice is the voice of Ya'akov, but the arms are the arms of Esav. Are you really Esav?" he asked.

"I am," Ya'akov lied.

Then Yitzhak blessed him. "I pray that God will make you rich and strong and you will become the leader of a big family." And Ya'akov left.

At that moment, Esav came home from hunting. He prepared the meat and came to his father.

"Father, sit up and eat the food I've prepared so you can bless me as you promised."

"Who are you?" Yitzhak asked in a puzzled manner.

"I am Esav, your firstborn son, who brings you food from the hunt."

Yitzhak's body started to shake and his voice got angry. "I have been fooled! Your brother pretended to be you and I gave HIM my blessings instead of you!"

"Bless me too! Have you not a blessing for me as well?" pleaded Esav. He did, but it was not the same blessing and it was too late. Ya'akov had been given the privilege of being the head of the household.

After that, Esav was so angry at his brother that he didn't speak to him. He even wanted to hurt him. Rivka told him he should go away to Haran, to stay at the house of his Uncle Laban until Esav felt less angry. And Ya'akov left for many years.

SONG (tune: "Mary Had a Little Lamb"—traditional)

Rivka and Yitzhak
They had twins (3x)
Rivka and Yitzhak
They had twins
Their names were Ya'akov and Esav.

Ya'akov liked to
cook and learn (3x)
Ya'akov liked to cook and learn
But Esav liked to hunt.

Rivka and Ya'akov
tricked Yitzhak (3x)
Rivka and Ya'akov tricked Yitzhak
Esav was very mad.

Esav was the older son, older son, older son
Esav was the older son
But Ya'akov was blessed first.

Ya'akov had to run away, run away, run away
Ya'akov had to run away
So he would not get hurt.

MULTIMEDIA IDEAS

"ASK ME" STICKER: Ask me why Ya'akov had to run away from Esav.

COOKING: Make vegetable soup:

Vegetable Soup

1 very large onion
½ of a bag of dried lentils (rinsed and checked for dirt)
1–3 cloves garlic (to taste)
1 large can peeled tomatoes
1 fairly large eggplant
2–3 zucchini
1 large green pepper
1 large yellow pepper
Olive oil, salt, paprika, to taste
Water or vegetable broth

1. Dice the veggies into 1-inch pieces. Crush the garlic.
2. Sauté the onion and peppers in olive oil until the onions are softened. Add eggplant, zucchini, and garlic and sauté some more. Add the tomatoes and lentils. Season with salt, paprika, and herbs. Fill the pot with water or vegetable broth. Simmer until the lentils and veggies are done and the soup smells yummy!

CRAFT: Make a double-sided Ya'akov and Esav puppet—one side smooth and one side hairy.

LANGUAGE: Talk about opposites (e.g., hairy and smooth, big and little, strong and weak)

DRAMA: Practice "hunting" with bows and arrows, targets, and other outdoor games.

Parashat Toldot Family Discussion

(from *Morah, Morah, Teach Me Torah*)

Toldot means "offspring." In this week's parashah we learn about the offspring of Rivka and Yitzhak.

Rivka and Yitzhak are very happy but are getting older and have no children. So they pray. God answers their prayers, and Rivka becomes pregnant. She is worried because there is so much tumult in her belly. So she prays again, and God tells her that she will have twin boys, both will become leaders, but the younger will rule the older. God will bless them both. After a while, Rivka has the babies; the first is born with lots of red hair (Esav/Esau) and the second (Ya'akov/Jacob) is born with smooth skin and is holding the heel of the first baby. Although they are twins, they are very different. Esav likes to hunt, and Ya'akov likes to cook and learn. After returning from hunting one day, Esav is so hungry that he offers to sell his birthright to Ya'akov for a bowl of lentil stew (seems like a good deal!). Now, because God told Rivka that the younger would rule the older, Rivka and Ya'akov trick Yitzhak into giving the firstborn son's blessing to Ya'akov instead of Esav (Yitzhak is blind, so they put goat skins on Ya'akov so he feels like Esav). When Esav returns home, he goes to get his blessing from his father, but it is too late! Esav is so angry that Ya'akov must leave town right away so he will not be hurt.

Family Discussion Questions:

1. (Q) Who are Rivka and Yitzhak's children? (A) Twins named Esav and Ya'akov.
2. (Q) Who did God say to Rivka would be the leader? (A) Ya'akov, the younger, will rule the older.
3. (Q) How did Ya'akov and Rikva trick Yitzhak? (A) Rivka put goat skins on Ya'akov's arms so he would resemble Esav and get the first blessing.

VA-YETZE

In last week's parashah Ya'akov had to leave Canaan and go to Haran to get away from his angry brother. He was afraid he would never see his family again. Esav was very angry, so Ya'akov needed to leave to stay safe.

In the parashah Va-Yetze, which means "departing," or "going away," Ya'akov began his travels.

(Get out your bride and groom dress-up clothes for acting out this parashah!)

He walked for a whole day and came to a place to rest for the night. He built a fire and made himself some food. He was all alone and was a little afraid so he sang himself a song.

SONG: "Twinkle, Twinkle *Kokhavim*"
(tune: "Twinkle, Twinkle Little Star"—traditional)

Twinkle, twinkle *kokhavim*
Way up in the *shamayim*
When I say the Shema by day, everything will be okay
When I say the Shema at night, everything will be all right.

Then he was able to go to sleep. He didn't have time to pack all the comforts of home when he ran away, so he used a rock for a pillow. That must have been very uncomfortable! That night he had a dream. There was a ladder stretching up to the sky. There were angels going up and down the ladder.

SONG (tune: "Hurry, Hurry, Drive Your Fire Truck"—traditional)

(Have the children pretend to climb a ladder and move their bodies up and down.)

We are climbing Ya'akov's ladder, we are climbing Ya'akov's ladder, we are climbing Ya'akov's ladder, angels of God.

We are climbing up and down, we are climbing up and down
We are climbing up and down, angels of God.

Then in his dream, God spoke to Ya'akov! "I am the Eternal, the God of Avraham, your grandfather, and the God of Yitzhak, your father. This ground where you lay is holy. But I give it to you and all your children. You will have as many children as there is dust on the earth. All the families of the earth shall be blessed through you. I will always be with you and I will bring you back to this land."

When Ya'akov awoke, he knew this place was holy. He poured some oil over the rock he used as a pillow, so he would always remember this place. He named the place Beth-El. Beth-El means "house of God."

He traveled many more days and came to a well. There were many flocks of sheep nearby. Then he saw a beautiful girl come to the well. She came to get water for her sheep, but she couldn't move the rock that covered the mouth of the well herself. Usually it took three men to move the rock, but Ya'akov moved it himself! He helped the girl water her flocks.

"Who are you?" asked Ya'akov.

"I am Rachel, the daughter of Laban," replied the girl.

Ya'akov hugged Rachel and said, "I am Ya'akov, the son of your father's sister. I have traveled very far to find you." Ya'akov immediately fell in love with Rachel.

They went back to Laban's house, and Ya'akov was introduced to Laban, Laban's wife, and Rachel's older sister, Leah. Ya'akov told Laban, "I love Rachel and want to marry her!"

Laban replied, "First you must work for me for seven years, and then you may marry Rachel."

So, Ya'akov worked for seven long years to marry the girl he loved. Then it was time for the wedding, a huge feast was prepared, and everyone got ready.

(Have the bride with a thick veil over her face, and have a groom under a tallit huppah.)

The bride was led out to the huppah with a beautiful lace veil over her face. They were married and had a beautiful party and then went to sleep. The next morning, Ya'akov woke up and looked at his beautiful bride. "Wait!" said Ya'akov. "You are not Rachel! You are Leah! I've been tricked!"

Ya'akov went to see Laban and said: "You tricked me, I worked seven years for the right to marry Rachel, and we had a deal. Instead, you gave me Leah. You broke your promise!"

"In our country, the older sister always marries first. Work for seven more years and then you may marry Rachel," replied Laban.

Ya'akov finally got to marry the woman he loved so much, his beloved Rachel.

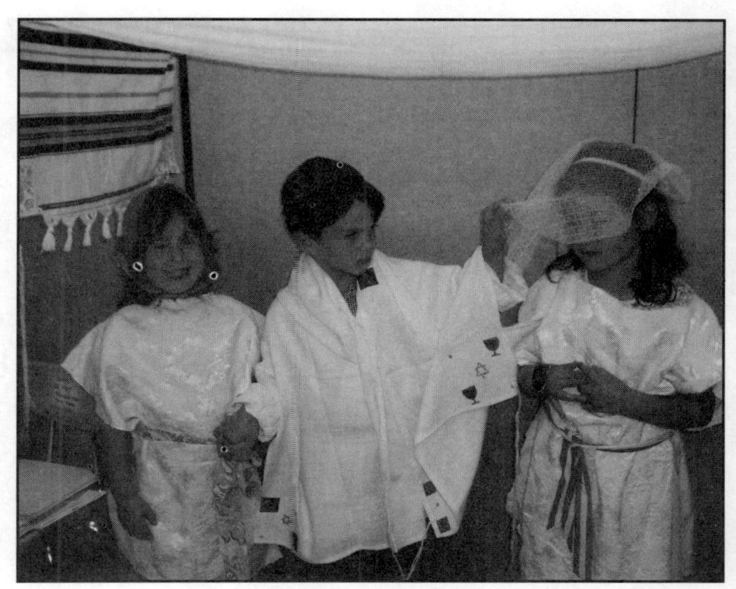

SONG (tune: "Here Comes the Bride"—traditional)

Here comes the bride, here comes the groom.
Ya'akov and Rachel will be married soon.
Ya'akov takes Rachel to be his wife.
Together they'll live a long, happy life.

As time went on, Ya'akov had twelve sons and one daughter. Ya'akov worked for many years (twenty!) for Laban and made Laban very rich.

Ya'akov said to Laban, "Now it is time for me to go home to my family in Canaan. Please let me take all the spotted and freckled animals from the flocks as payment for all my years of work."

Laban agreed. God blessed the flocks, and suddenly all the animals were having spotted and freckled babies! So Laban changed his mind and said. "No, I want you to take only the pure white animals for yourself." He could see there were more spotted and freckled animals. Now suddenly all the animals were having only pure white babies! God appeared to Laban in a dream and said, "Do not do anything to Ya'akov!" Laban realized that God only blessed what Ya'akov was supposed to get! Laban gave Ya'akov all the freckled and spotted animals and allowed Ya'akov to leave Haran with his flocks, his wives, and his children.

MULTIMEDIA IDEAS

"ASK ME" STICKER: Ask me who Ya'akov wanted to marry? (Rachel)

DRAMA: Act out a wedding scene. Use a veil you can't see through. Practice walking around the groom seven times.

COOKING: Have a wedding feast. Bake a wedding cake!

MATH: (1) Practice counting. Make groups of seven things.

(2) Using play animals, create categories of spotted animals versus non-spotted animals, and count them.

MOVEMENT: With masking tape, make a ladder on the floor. Have the children practice being the angels of God going up and down, jumping through the rungs, hopping, side-stepping, etc.

SONG (tune: "The Wheels on the Bus"—traditional)

Ya'akov went to see Laban, see Laban, see Laban.
Ya'akov went to see Laban, and fell in love with Rachel.

Ya'akov worked for seven years, seven years, seven years.
Ya'akov worked for seven years so he could marry Rachel.

But Laban tricked Ya'akov, Ya'akov, Ya'akov.
Laban tricked Ya'akov, he married Leah instead.

So, Ya'akov worked seven years more,
Seven years more, seven years more.

Ya'akov worked seven years more
And finally married Rachel.

Parashat Va-Yetze Family Discussion

(from *Morah, Morah, Teach Me Torah*)

The word *va-yetze* means "and he departed." Ya'akov departed from his home because Esav was very angry with him. He got ready to camp out for the night and used a rock for his pillow. That night Ya'akov had a dream about a ladder reaching way up to the sky. There were angels climbing up and down the ladder. In his dream, God spoke to Ya'akov and said, "This ground is holy, but I give it to you and your children. You will have as many children as there is dust on the earth. All families of the earth will be blessed through you. I will always be with you, and I will bring you back to this land."

When Ya'akov awoke, he knew the place where he lay was holy. He poured oil over the rock he slept on and named the place Beth-El (house of God). He got ready to continue on his journey.

Ya'akov arrived at a well and saw a beautiful girl. There was a rock covering the mouth of the well that usually took three people to move. Ya'akov moved the rock himself to help the girl water her flocks. Who was the girl? Rachel! Rachel's father, Laban, told Ya'akov that if he worked for seven years he could marry Rachel. But under the *ḫuppah*, Ya'akov was tricked into marrying Rachel's older sister, Leah. After seven more years, Ya'akov finally got to marry Rachel. After living with Laban for twenty years, Ya'akov packed up and went home to see his family.

Family Discussion Questions:

1. (Q) What did Ya'akov sleep on? (A) A rock.
2. (Q) What did he name the holy place? (A) Beth-El.
3. (Q) Whom did Ya'akov meet? (A) Rachel.
4. (Q) God said that Ya'akov would return to the land. What land do you think that is? (A) Canaan, or Israel.

VA-YISHLAH

Last week we read about Ya'akov marrying both Rachel and Leah. He and his brother had been separated for a long time. Now it was time for him to return home.

In this week's parashah, Va-Yishlah, which means "to send away", we learn that Ya'akov had been in Haran for twenty years! He was so happy to return to Canaan, the home of his mother, his father, and his twin brother, Esav. Ya'akov and his family packed all their belongings. They began their trip back to Canaan. Ya'akov was worried that maybe Esav would still be angry with him, even after all these years.

"I had such a big fight with my brother and I hope, with God's help, we will find a way to be friends again and live peacefully together," said Ya'akov.

(To act out this parashah, have some children dressed as animals and some as Ya'akov's family and walk around the room together carrying all their possessions.)

They walked and walked. That night, they stopped to rest and set up camp near a stream. They spread out blankets and built a fire, so they could eat and get ready for bed.

Ya'akov called over several of his shepherds. "Gather some men and some of my best sheep, goats, and cows. I want you to go ahead of me to meet Esav and give him all these gifts from me. God has blessed me with many gifts, and I want to share them with my brother." The men did as they were told.

Soon everyone was asleep, everyone except Ya'akov. During the night a stranger came upon Ya'akov. They began to struggle. They fought all night long. Ya'akov hurt his hip. As the sun started coming up, the stranger stopped fighting and said, "You have wrestled all night with an angel of God and won! Your name is Ya'akov, meaning the heel holder, but from now on your name will be Yisrael [Israel], one who wrestles with God."

SONG (tune: "He Waded in the Water and He Got His Ankles Wet" or "John Brown's Body"—traditional)

Ya'akov met an angel and they wrestled all night long (3x)
And Ya'akov hurt his hip

The angel changed Ya'akov's name (3x)
His name is now Yisrael

During the night Ya'akov's servants came upon Esav and gave him the gifts from Ya'akov. "Please, I don't need any gifts from my brother; I also have been blessed with many things. Just bring my brother to me!" said Esav. The servants could see that Esav was no longer angry and went to get Ya'akov.

The brothers ran to each other and hugged each other! "I'm so happy to see you. I've missed you so much these past years!" said Ya'akov.

"I am happy to see you, too!" said Esav. Although they reunited, they were never really friends.

MULTIMEDIA IDEAS

"ASK ME" STICKER: Ask me what Ya'akov's new name is. (Yisrael)

LANGUAGE: Talk about different ways to solve problems with our friends.

TZEDAKAH PROJECT: Just as Ya'akov gave gifts to Esav, you also could make some gifts to give to an area nursing home. Examples: Make paper flowers, decorate pots and plant flowers in the pots, bake cookies, etc.

CRAFT: Make a picture of all the things you would give to a sibling if you had a fight and didn't see each other for a long, long time (either items from that era [e.g., camels, goats, sheep, fruit, grain] or from your child's world [e.g., toys, books, candy, hugs])

Parashat Va-Yishlah Family Discussion

(from *Morah, Morah, Teach Me Torah*)

Va-yishlah means "and he sent." Ya'akov has been in Haran, away from his family, for twenty years. He is heading home with his wives and children and all of his flocks of animals. As they get ready to camp for the night, he decides to send some of his shepherds ahead with gifts for Esav. He hopes that Esav is not still angry after all these years, and Ya'akov would like to share some of the things that God has blessed him with.

Then everyone goes to sleep. Ya'akov is awoken by a stranger, and they struggle all night long. Ya'akov injures his hip. As the sun comes up, the stranger stops wrestling and tells Ya'akov (meaning "heel holder") that he has wrestled with an angel of God and that God will change his name to Yisrael (meaning "one who wrestled with God").

The next day, Ya'akov met up with his brother and they hugged. Although they reunited, they were never really friends.

Family Discussion Questions:

1. (Q) How long did Ya'akov live in Haran? (A) Twenty years.
2. (Q) What happened to Ya'akov during the night? (A) He wrestled with an angel and had his name changed to Yisrael.
3. (Q) Did Ya'akov see his twin brother Esav again? (A) Yes.
4. (Q) Was Esav still angry? (A) No.
5. (Q) If you had an argument with your brother or sister, how did you make up?

VA-YESHEV

In last week's parashah Ya'akov and Esav were reunited. Ya'akov met an angel and his name was changed to Yisrael. In Va-Yeshev we learn again that Ya'akov has a new name, Yisrael (Israel, in English). He returns to Canaan and lives a full life with his family. Yisrael has twelve sons and one daughter. His favorite sons are Yosef (Joseph) and Binyamin (Benjamin). They are Rachel's sons. How would you feel if your parents had a favorite child?

This week we read the parashat Va-Yeshev, which means "settled"—Ya'akov settled in his father's land of Canaan. Ya'akov gave his favorite son Yosef (Joseph) a very special coat. The coat had many different colors and was very beautiful.

SONG 1) "Colors in My World" by Judy Caplan Ginsburgh from the CD *My Jewish World*

Chorus: There are colors all around, colors like a rainbow, lots of colors in my world. There are colors all around, colors like a rainbow, lots of colors in my world.

There's *kahol* (blue) for the sky, where the birds fly way up high. There's *kahol* for the sky, lots of colors in my world.

There's *tzahov* (yellow) for the sun, when it shines we play and have fun. There's *tzahov* for the sun, lots of colors in my world.

There's *yarok* (green) for the grass, where we really shouldn't throw trash. There's *yarok* for the grass, lots of colors in my world.

There's *adom* (red) for the flowers, they grow tall when the rain showers. There's *adom* for the flowers, lots of colors in my world.

SONG 2) "The Color Song" by Carol Boyd Leon from the CD *Gan Shirim*

Ka<u>h</u>ol (blue) is the color I see. *ka<u>h</u>ol* looks good to me!
When I look up at the sky, *ka<u>h</u>ol* is what I see. Oh,

Lavan (white) is the color I see. *Lavan* looks good to me!
When I watch the falling snow, *lavan* is what I see. Oh,

Adom (red) is the color I see. *Adom* looks good to me!
When I look at a strawberry, *adom* is what I see. Oh,

Yarok (green) is the color I see. *Yarok* looks good to me!
When I look down at the grass, *yarok* is what I see. Oh,

Tzahov (yellow) is the color I see. *Tzahov* looks good to me!
When the school bus passes by, *tzahov* is what I see. Oh,

Katom (orange) is the color I see. *Katom* looks good to me!
When I'm in the pumpkin patch, *katom* is what I see. Oh,

Sha<u>h</u>or (black) is the color I see. *Sha<u>h</u>or* looks good to me!
When I watch the tires go round, *sha<u>h</u>or* is what I see. Oh,

Kesef (silver) is the color I see. *Kesef* looks good to me!
When I look at the kiddush cup, *kesef* is what I see. Oh,

Zahav is the color I see. *Zahav* looks good to me!
When I see Queen Esther's crown, *zahav* is what I see.

Yosef's brothers were very jealous and upset that Yosef received such a special gift from their dad.

"Why didn't I get the special coat? I work the hardest." asked Levi.

"What about me? I'm the oldest!" shouted Reuven.

They were all grumbling as they headed out to the fields with the flocks.

Yosef loved his special coat. He didn't even notice his brothers' anger. Yosef was different from his brothers; he liked to cook and learn (just like his dad!). He didn't help with the hunting or with taking care of the flocks. This also made the brothers angry.

One night Yosef had two dreams. In one dream there were eleven bundles of grain bowing down to one bundle of grain. In the other dream, there was the sun, the moon and eleven stars all bowing down to him! He told his brothers about the dreams. They were furious! They hated him even more.

"How dare you! Are you saying we should bow down to you?" The brothers were so angry they stormed off to the fields to take care of the flocks.

As evening came, Ya'akov sent Yosef out to the fields to get his brothers for dinner. Yosef's brothers could see him approaching and came up with a plan. They would throw Yosef into a nearby pit. They tore off his beautiful coat and threw him into the pit.

"Help me!" yelled Yosef. But the brothers just laughed at him.

Some of his brother's wanted to kill him, but Reuven said, "No! Yosef is very special to our father. We must have respect for our father!"

Just then a group of traveling merchants came by, and the brothers decided to sell Yosef to the merchants! So Yosef was brought to Egypt and placed in Pharaoh's palace as a slave, working for Potiphar.

Meanwhile, the brothers had to tell their father something! What would they say? They took Yosef's coat and put goat's blood on it. The brother's lied to their father and said, "This was all we found of Yosef's." Ya'akov was so upset that he started to cry. "No! Yosef must have been killed by wild animals! Not my favorite son!" wailed Ya'akov.

Meanwhile, Yosef was working in Pharaoh's palace in Egypt. He worked very hard but somehow got into trouble and was sent to jail, even though it wasn't his fault! He lived in the jail for many years.

While he was in jail, he met Pharaoh's butler and baker. One night they each had a dream. With God's help, Yosef was able to tell the butcher and the baker what their dreams meant, and they came true! Yosef begged them to remember how he was able to help them with their dreams. "Remember me! Maybe I can help you again one day, when you are in the palace." said Yosef.

Who knows, maybe he will!

MULTIMEDIA IDEAS

"ASK ME" STICKER: Ask me who was given a beautiful coat of many colors. (Yosef)

LANGUAGE: Discuss Yosef's beautiful coat of many colors; talk about colors in English, Hebrew, and American Sign Language. When you sing the ASL color song, either use ASL signs for the colors or cut out construction paper color sheets for each child to hold up during the song. ASL color signs are available at www.lifeprint.com/asl101/pages-signs/b/blue.htm

SONG/MOVEMENT: **ASL (Signing) "Color Song" (tune: "Tapuhim U'Dvash—Israeli traditional; or "Apples and Honey" by Judith Caplan Ginsburgh)**

If you're wearing brown, jump up and down.
If you're wearing brown, jump up and down.
Now, show me the sign, show me the sign.
If you're wearing brown, jump up and down.

If you're wearing purple, turn in a circle.
If you're wearing purple, turn in a circle.
Now, show me the sign, show me the sign.
If you're wearing purple, turn in a circle.

If you're wearing red, stand and touch your head.
If you're wearing red, stand and touch your head.
Now, show me the sign, show me the sign.
If you're wearing red, stand and touch your head.

If you're wearing pink, try and wink.
If you're wearing pink, try and wink.
Now, show me the sign, show me the sign.
If you're wearing pink, try and wink.

If you're wearing blue, bend and touch your shoe.
If you're wearing blue, bend and touch your shoe.
Now, show me the sign, show me the sign.
If you're wearing blue, bend and touch your shoe.

If you're wearing yellow, act like some Jell-O.
If you're wearing yellow, act like some Jell-O.
Now, show me the sign, show me the sign.
If you're wearing yellow, act like some Jell-O.

If you're wearing white, give me a fright—BOO!
If you're wearing white, give me a fright—BOO!
Now, show me the sign, show me the sign.
If you're wearing white, give me a fright—BOO!

If you're wearing green, make your face real mean.
If you're wearing green, make your face real mean.
Now, show me the sign, show me the sign.
If you're wearing green, make your face real mean.
Now SIT!

SCIENCE: Practice mixing colors and see what you get! This is also fun to do by mixing different colors of kosher gelatin or whipped cream (like Rich's Whip) with food coloring in ziplock bags and squishing them together to see the colors change. Plus you can eat your finished product! (Carmel makes kosher gelatin.)

CRAFT: Draw designs with washable markers on coffee filters. Using a spray bottle filled with water, spray the filters and watch the colors bleed and mix. After it dries, you can cut it into the shape of a coat and place on a paper doll. Discuss how they would have made colors in those days. (They used fruits and vegetables and vegetation that grew in the land. Go outside and gather articles of nature and try to rub them onto paper or fabric to make colors.)

FAMILY CORNER: Tie-dye a pillowcase to create a coat for Yosef to keep in your dress-up area (food coloring works well—use gloves!).

Parashat Va-Yeshev Family Discussion

(from *Morah, Morah, Teach Me Torah*)

Va-Yeshev means "settled." Ya'akov is settled back in his homeland of Canaan with his two wives, twelve sons, and daughter. His favorite son is Yosef (Joseph—Rachel's son). In this week's parashah, Ya'akov gives his favorite son a beautiful coat with many colors. This causes a lot of jealousy and hurt feelings among the other brothers. They begin to hate Yosef. One night, Yosef has a dream where eleven bundles of grain bow down to one bundle of grain. Then he has another dream where the sun, moon, and eleven stars bow down to him. He tells his brothers about the dreams, and they become very angry. They decide to put him in a pit and sell him as a slave. Ya'akov is devastated, as he thinks Yosef is dead. Instead, Yosef ends up in Egypt in Pharaoh's palace working for Potiphar, Pharaoh's helper. Yosef has been given a special gift from God to be able to understand dreams. Yosef gets into trouble with Potiphar's wife and ends up in jail. In jail, Yosef is able to tell two of Pharaoh's men what their dreams mean, and they come true. Yosef tells them, "Don't forget about me!"

Family Discussion Questions

1. (Q) Who was Ya'akov's favorite son? (A) Yosef.
2. (Q) Did his brothers like that Yosef was the favorite? (A) No!
3. (Q) What happened to Yosef? (A) He was sold as a slave and ended up in an Egyptian jail.
4. (Q) What was Yosef's special gift? (A) He could tell people what their dreams meant.

MIKETZ

Last week we learned that Yosef was Ya'akov's favorite son and he was given a coat of many colors. This week we read Miketz, which means "it happened," and we read more about Yosef's dreams. Yosef always knew what his dreams meant, and he could tell what the dreams of others meant. One day, the king of Egypt, Pharaoh, awoke in the middle of the night frightened; he had a dream that puzzled him. He called for his magicians and his advisors to come to his room.

"I've had a strange dream. I don't know what it means. Do you know who can tell me what this dream means?"

They could not explain his dreams.

"There is someone who can interpret your dreams. Unfortunately, he is in jail right now," they said.

"Who is this person? Take him out of jail and bring him to me, and I will tell him my dreams. I must find out the meaning of my dreams!" Pharaoh exclaimed.

"His name is Yosef, and we will bring him here," they told the king.

When Yosef arrived at Pharaoh's palace, Pharaoh ordered him to listen to his dreams and to tell him what they meant.

"Please, Your Excellency, tell me your dreams, and with God's help, I will tell you what they mean," answered Yosef.

Pharaoh began telling his dreams: "I was standing by the river, and I saw seven fat cows. They were eating grass near the water. All of the sudden seven very thin, sickly cows came and began to eat the seven fat cows. I was so frightened that I woke up, but when I fell asleep again, I had another dream. This time I saw seven full ears of corn next to seven scraggly, thin ears of corn. The seven thin ears of corn ate up the seven full ears of corn. I have told these dreams to everyone, but no one can tell me what they mean."

"Well," said Yosef, "both dreams mean the same thing. It means that you will have seven rich years with lots of food to eat and lots of crops in Egypt. Then you will have seven bad years, seven years of no rain and bad crops, and everyone will be hungry."

"What should I do?" the king asked.

"First you must tell the people to store up as much food as they can during the seven good years so they will be able to live and eat during the seven bad years," Yosef answered.

The king believed Yosef. "You are a wise man, and I will do as you say. You can live in my palace with me, and you will be a very important leader in Egypt."

Things happened just as Yosef predicted. Not only were things bad in Egypt, but in Canaan, where Yosef's father Ya'akov lived, there were hard times as well. The people were hungry; they didn't know what to do. Finally, Ya'akov said to his sons, "Leave and go to Egypt, and ask Pharaoh to allow us to buy food."

SONG (tune: "I'm a Little Teapot"—Traditional)

There was a boy named Yosef.
He was Ya'akov and Rachel's son
He got a special coat
'cause he's the favorite son.

Yosef understood dreams
And he got his brothers mad
They sold him as a slave
Oy, that was very bad!

Yosef went to work
As Pharaoh's right hand man
He read Pharaoh's dreams
Then he saved the land.

The most shocking sight
That Yosef had seen,
His brothers bowing down to him
Just like in his dream!

When Yosef sees his brothers he can't believe his eyes! They are all there, bowing down before him, just like in his dream so many years ago. Only the youngest brother Binyamin is missing. Yosef's brothers do not recognize him. He must find out if his father and brother are still alive! So Yosef tests his brothers to see if they have changed their ways and have become kind. He asks, "Who are you? Are you spies?"

"No," replies Reuven, "we are brothers. Our father and youngest brother are home in Canaan, and we have no food. We've traveled a long distance to ask if you will please sell us food."

"How do I know that you are really brothers? I will keep the oldest son, and the rest of you return with your youngest brother. Then I will give you food."

After some time, the brothers did return to Egypt with the youngest son. Binyamin was very afraid. Yosef tested his brothers again, by putting a kiddush cup into Binyamin's sack of grain so it looked as if he stole it.

MULTIMEDIA IDEAS

"ASK ME" STICKER: Ask me who helped tell Pharaoh what his dreams meant? (Yosef)

LANGUAGE: Write a story about your dreams and try to interpret them. What do the children think they mean?

MATH: The number seven is important in this parashah (e.g. seven fat cows and seven skinny cows). Make a list of all the things that include the number seven: i.e., seven branches on the menorah, seven days of the week, seven brakhot in a wedding, *hakafot* (marching seven times around the Torah on Simhat Torah).

DRAMATIC PLAY: Set up a store with grains, fruits, and vegetables so the children can take turns selling the food to the hungry people.

COOKING: Cook something that uses grains (e.g., tabouleh, corn bread, couscous, bread). You could also sort and do patterns using different kinds of grains (e.g., corn, wheat berries, oats).

Parashat Miketz Family Discussion

(from *Morah, Morah, Teach Me Torah*)

Miketz means "it happened." We learned last week that Yosef knew how to tell what dreams meant. It happened that Pharaoh had two dreams that were haunting him. He dreamed of seven fat ears of corn and seven very thin ears of corn. The skinny ears ate the fat ears. Then he dreamed of seven fat cows and seven skinny cows. The skinny cows ate the fat cows. No one knew what these dreams meant. Then a person who worked for Pharaoh remembered about Yosef in jail, how he told them what their dream meant and it came true. Pharaoh sent for Yosef right away. Yosef told Pharaoh that his two dreams meant the same thing. In Egypt, there would be seven years with plenty of rain and crops, and seven years of famine. He told Pharaoh that in order to save Egypt, he needed to save food during the seven good years so everyone could eat during the seven bad years. Pharaoh made Yosef his new helper and put him in charge of the project. After the seven years of plenty, the famine came. Things were bad not only in Egypt, but in Canaan as well. Yosef's brothers came to buy food from him and bowed down before him. They did not recognize Yosef, but he recognized them. He wanted to make sure his brothers were kinder people now than they were when he lived with them, so he tested them by asking them to bring their youngest brother (Binyamin [Benjamin], also Rachel's son, like Yosef) to Egypt. So the brothers returned with Binyamin and Yosef tested the brothers again by placing a kiddush cup in Binyamin's bag of grain so it looked as if he stole it.

Family Discussion Questions:

1. (Q) What did Pharaoh's dreams mean? (A) Seven years with lots of rain and crops, and seven years with no rain and no crops.
2. (Q) How did Yosef save Egypt? (A) He stored grain during the seven years with lots of crops and sold it during the seven years when nothing grew.
3. (Q) Do you think Yosef's brothers will be kinder now?

VA-YIGASH

In last week's parashah, Yosef's brothers return and bow down before him, just like he saw in his dream. Remember that Yosef tests his brothers by putting a kiddush cup into Binyamin's bag? In this week's parashah, Va-Yigash, which means "approaches," Yehudah (Judah) approaches Yosef to beg him to let his brother Binyamin go. The brothers still don't recognize Yosef as their long-lost brother, and Yosef decides to test his brothers once again. He asks to check inside the bag. What did he find?

"Thief!" yells Yosef. "Guards, put the youngest brother into jail immediately!"

"NO!" shout all the brothers at once. "Take me instead!" yells Reuven. "No! Take me instead!" says Simeon. "No!" says Levi, "Take me instead!"

All the brothers fought over who would go to jail instead of Binyamin!

"Why do you protect your brother so?" asked Yosef.

"We lost another brother once, and it hurt our father terribly. We never want to hurt our father again. You see, Binyamin is the youngest and the favorite child. Please don't hurt our father. He is an old man and has suffered enough," explained Reuven.

Suddenly Yosef begins to cry. "I am your brother you sold as a slave so many years ago! Don't you recognize me? God sent me ahead of you to save people's lives. Please, go get our father and the family and come live with me here!"

So, the brothers return and tell Ya'akov everything. He is so happy he begins to cry! The family goes to Egypt to live with their long, lost-brother Yosef.

SONG (tune: "We're Going to Kentucky, We're Going to the Fair"—traditional)

You must leave Canaan today
You'll go to Egypt I say
And go to the king and ask for food
So our strength can be renewed.

The brothers leave for Egypt now
They'll get there somehow
They're hungry and they're very sad
Oh things are very bad.

When the brothers got to Egypt
They walked up to the king
And brother Yosef was standing there
He recognized his siblings.

MULTIMEDIA IDEAS

"ASK ME" STICKER: Ask me why Yosef tests his brothers.

CRAFT: Look at different kiddush cups and talk about the different designs on them. Then design your own kiddush cup.

MOVEMENT: Play "team" type games where the children must work together. Have the children get into pairs and sit back-to-back. Have them link their arms together and try to stand up and walk. If that is too easy, try with three or four kids!

GAME: Take five margarine containers with lids and label them one through five. Cut a small hole in the top of each lid (about the size of a dime). Use tweezers to have the children put corn kernels into each container to match the number on each lid. Great for fine motor skills! Or get out the sand table or rice table, and using measuring cups, practice filling up containers of "grain."

Parashat Va-Yigash Family Discussion

(from *Morah, Morah, Teach Me Torah*)

Last week Yosef placed a kiddush cup into Binyamin's bag of grain. In Parashat Va-Yigash, which means "approaches," the brothers approach Yosef and bow down before him. They still do not recognize their brother they sold as a slave so many years ago. Yosef tests his brothers with the kiddush cup. How will they react when Yosef tries to put Binyamin into jail for stealing? All the brothers beg Yosef at once to take them instead of their youngest brother. When Yosef asks why, the brothers explain that they lost a brother once and never want to hurt their father again. Yosef starts to cry and reveals his true identity to his brothers, saying, "I am the brother you sold as a slave so many years ago. God sent me ahead of you to save lives." Yosef knows that everything was God's plan and sends for his father, Ya'akov, to come and join them in the palace. So Ya'akov and his whole large family pack up and leave Canaan to go to Egypt to be with Yosef, where there is plenty of food.

Family Discussion Questions:

1. (Q) Why did Yosef test his brothers? (A) To see if they were kinder than they were to Yosef.
2. (Q) Did the brothers change their attitudes toward each other? (A) Yes.
3. (Q) How do you think the brothers reacted when Yosef told his brothers who he really was?

VA-YEHI

Last week we read Va-Yigash, where Yosef and his family were reunited. This week's parashah, Va-Yehi, which means "and he lived," is very important because it is the last parashah or chapter in the book of Bereshit (Genesis). Remember that there are five books of the Torah and we will finish reading the first book! (See the "Five Books" song in the Children's Introduction on page 9.)

Ya'akov and his family had been living in Egypt for many years. Ya'akov was very old, 147 years old. and he knew he would soon die. So he called for his son Yosef to come to him. He said to Yosef, "I want you to promise me something. Egypt is not the land where I came from. When I die, I want to be buried in the land of Canaan, near my fathers. I want to be buried in the Cave of Makhpelah. God has come to me and blessed me and told me our families will grow into a large community and the Land of Canaan would be our homeland."

"Yes, I promise I will do what you ask," Yosef replied.

"Now I want to bless your two sons, Menashe and Ephraim. Bring them to me," said Ya'akov.

Ephraim, the younger son of Yosef, stood next to his older brother Menashe, and Ya'akov placed his old, weak arms on their heads. It was the custom in that time to put the right hand on the older child's head to give a blessing. But Ya'akov crisscrossed his hands and placed his right hand on the younger son Ephraim and his left hand on Menashe, the older son, therefore giving the special blessing to the younger son. Remember when Ya'akov, the younger son of Yitzhak, was blessed first instead of Esav?

"God, bless these boys as You have blessed Avraham, Yitzhak, and myself, and let them grow as a great nation on the Earth."

Later on, when the Torah talks about the twelve tribes of Israel, Ephraim and Menashe were each counted as a tribe.

Ya'akov called for his own sons to come and be blessed as well. Then he died. (There is a midrash that says when Ya'akov was about to die, he told his sons he was worried about leaving them in a land where the people pray to idols. The sons said, *"Shema Yisrael Adonai Eloheinu, Adonai EHAD*! Listen Yisrael, God is our God, God is ONE!" And Ya'akov replied, "Blessed be God's name forever. *Barukh shem k'vod malkhuto l'olam va'ed.*")

Since that time, parents have blessed their children on Shabbat and holidays.

To our sons, we say,

יְשִׂמְךָ אֱלֹהִים כְּאֶפְרַיִם וְכִמְנַשֶּׁה.

"May God bless you like Ephraim and Menashe."

And to our daughters, we say,

יְשִׂמֵךְ אֱלֹהִים כְּשָׂרָה רִבְקָה רָחֵל וְלֵאָה.

"May God bless you like our mothers, Sarah, Rivka, Rachel, and Leah."

Yosef continued to live in Egypt with his brothers. He was never angry at them for selling him as a slave, because God had a plan. God sent Yosef ahead to save his family's lives. Yosef lived to be 110 years old. Before he died, God told Yosef that God would not forget the Jewish people. God would take the Jewish people out of Egypt and God would take care of them.

At the end of each of the five books of Torah we say: *Hazak, hazak, v'nit-hazek*! Be strong, be strong, and be strengthened!

SONG (tune: "Mary Had A Little Lamb"—traditional)

Hazak, hazak, v'nit-hazek, v'nit-hazek, v'nit-hazek.
Hazak, hazak, v'nit-hazek—be brave and be strong.

We read five books of the Torah, the Torah, the Torah.
We read five books of the Torah and then we say *hazak*.

Now we finished Bereshit, Bereshit, Bereshit.
Now we finished Bereshit and so we say *hazak*.

Hazak, hazak, v'nit-hazek, v'nit-hazek, v'nit-hazek.
Hazak, hazak, v'nit-hazek—be brave and be strong.

MULTIMEDIA IDEAS

"ASK ME" STICKER: Ask me what we say when we finish reading a book of the Torah. (*Hazak*!)

DRAMATIC PLAY/SCIENCE: Build a cave like Makhpelah (papier-mâché) and learn about caves.

MATH: Ya'akov had twelve sons. Practice counting to twelve. Talk about what a dozen is. Create categories of things in groups of twelve (twelve farm animals, twelve little people, twelve pieces of candy.)

DISCUSSION: Yosef promises his father to bury him in Canaan. Talk about making and keeping promises. List promises that you have made. Did you keep them? Has anyone ever promised you something and not kept their promise? How did you feel?

SONG (traditional)

Shabbat is here, Shabbat is here.
I'm so glad that Shabbat is here.
Candles burning bright, it's Friday night.
I'm so glad that Shabbat is here.

Shabbat Shalom to ________ , *Shabbat Shalom* to ________ , etc. (As you sing the song, touch each child's head and sing their name, like we bless the children on Friday night.)

And have a good Shabbat!

Parashat Va-Yehi Family Discussion

(from *Morah, Morah, Teach Me Torah*)

The word *va-yehi* means "and he lived." Ya'akov and his family lived in Egypt for a long time. Ya'akov was 147 years old; he knew he would soon die, so he called together all his sons. He told Yosef that he wanted to be buried in Canaan in the Cave of Makhpelah. He told Yosef that God had blessed him, that his family would continue to grow and that the land of Canaan was to be their homeland. Yosef promised to do as Ya'akov asked. Ya'akov then asked to see Yosef's two sons, Menashe (the oldest) and Ephraim (the youngest) so he could bless them. Ya'akov crossed his hands and placed his right hand on the youngest son's head and his left hand on the older son's head. At that time, the oldest always got the right-handed blessing as the firstborn son. But just as Ya'akov received the firstborn son's blessing instead of his older brother, Esav, so did Ephraim receive the firstborn son's blessing instead of his older brother, Menashe. Ya'akov then blessed his twelve sons and died. When we bless our children on Friday nights, we say, "May God make you like Ephraim and Menashe, and like Sarah, Rivka, Rachel, and Leah." Yosef and the family continued to live in Egypt, although they knew they would return to Canaan one day. This is the last parashah in the book of Bereshit. *Hazak*!

Family Discussion Questions:

1. (Q) What did Ya'akov tell Yosef about the land of Canaan? (A) That it was meant to be their homeland.
2. (Q) How did Ya'akov bless Yosef's sons, Menashe and Ephraim? (A) He crossed his hands so the right hand was on the younger son's head.
3. (Q) After the blessing of the children on Shabbat, think of a blessing you can say to your parents on Shabbat.

SHEMOT

We are about to begin reading the second book of the Torah. It is called Shemot (which means "names"); in English it is referred to as the book of Exodus. Yosef (Joseph) lived in Egypt a long time, as did his children and all the children of Ya'akov (Jacob). They all had children and their children had children, and the Jewish people became a large group. Yosef finally died and the Pharaoh died. A new Pharaoh came into power to take the place of the old Pharaoh. This Pharaoh didn't know Yosef or his family; he didn't know how helpful Yosef had been. This Pharaoh also wasn't very nice. He looked at all the Children of Israel (the Jewish people) and saw how many of them there were. He was afraid that some day they would be more powerful than he was, so he decided to make enemies of them, to do everything in his power to make life terrible for the Jewish people. So he made them his slaves, making them do hard work, like building pyramids and cities for him. He assigned his taskmasters to watch over them to make sure they were working night and day.

SONG (tune: "Johnny Works with One Hammer"—traditional)

Pharaoh made the Jews work hard, work hard, work hard
Pharaoh made the Jews work hard
They worked so hard all day.

First they had to make bricks, make bricks, make bricks
First they had to make bricks
They worked so hard all day.

The Jews were building pyramids, pyramids, pyramids
The Jews were building pyramids
They worked so hard all day.

But this did not stop the Jews from having more and more children. They did not become weak as Pharaoh had hoped. So the king made a proclamation that all the Jewish baby boys would be taken away and put in the river to be drowned. He sent his spies to watch the Israelites so they would know where the baby boys were.

There was one Hebrew woman who was able to hide her baby son. Her name was Yokheved. She hid him for three months, but she knew that Pharaoh's spies would find him. She had a plan. She went out to the river and collected reeds that grew along the banks of the Nile River. With the reeds, she wove a basket. She spread tar inside the basket so it would be dry inside and would not sink. She put her baby into the basket and told her daughter, Miriam, to take the baby down to the river and put the basket in the river. "Make sure you follow the basket. Watch over your brother. Make sure he is safe," Yokheved told Miriam.

The Pharaoh's daughter, Batya, came to the river to bathe and she saw the basket with the baby. She lifted the basket out of the river. "Look! There is a baby in this basket. I'll bet he is a Hebrew baby. His mother must have left him here. I will take this baby home with me and care for him, but I will need a nursemaid to help care for him. Where should I find such a person?"

Miriam, who was standing close by, hiding in the reeds, came out. "I know of a nursemaid who can take care of this baby. I will run and get her."

"Very well," said the princess. "I will name this baby "Moshe [Moses], because Moshe means "to take out of the water."

SONG (tune: "The Farmer in the Dell"—traditional)

Who's floating in the Nile? (2x)
There's a baby crying, he must have been there a while.
The princess came to swim (2x)
She heard the baby crying, she took care of him.
Out of the water he came (2x)
She brought him from the water, and Moshe was his name.

Yokheved was so happy that someone found her son and ran to take care of him. He was raised in the palace until he grew up and became a man.

One day while Moshe was outside, he saw one of Pharaoh's taskmasters beating a Hebrew slave. Moshe ran over and said, "Stop beating this man; you're hurting him!" When the man would not stop beating the slave, Moshe became so angry that he ran over and hit the taskmaster. Moshe was afraid that the Pharaoh would be mad at him so he ran away. He went to the town of Midian, and he became a shepherd. He married a woman named Tzipporah. One day as he was tending his sheep, he saw a bush that was on fire, yet the leaves were not burnt. He approached the burning bush, and he heard a voice speaking to him. Who do you think will speak to Moshe? We'll find out next week!

MULTIMEDIA IDEAS

"ASK ME" STICKER: Ask me who was saved from the Nile River. (Moshe)

DRAMATIC PLAY: Turn your family corner into Egypt. Have a blue blanket Nile River, a baby doll in a basket, and costumes for Miriam, Yokheved, and the princess.

LARGE MOTOR SKILLS AND COOPERATIVE PLAY: Build pyramids out of blocks together.

SCIENCE: Make a baby Moshe out of craft foam (or you can use a little baby doll) and a basket out of a Styrofoam bowl, and float baby Moshe in your water table. Practice floating and sinking experiments.

CRAFT: Make a burning bush mural using red, orange green, and yellow tissue paper and brown for the trunk. Add painted pyramids and the Nile River to create the feeling of Egypt in your classroom.

LANGUAGE: Discuss the differences between being a slave and being a person of royalty (princess, Pharaoh); examples: homes, clothing, foods, work, etc.). Chart the differences.

SONG: Since we are starting a new book in the Torah, review the "Five Books" song found in the Children's Introduction (page 9).

Parashat Shemot Family Discussion

(from *Morah, Morah, Teach Me Torah*)

This is the first parashah in the second book of the Torah. Yosef had died and a new Pharaoh was now ruling Egypt. This Pharaoh was not kind and did not know how Yosef saved Egypt. He made the Jewish people work very hard building cities. Pharaoh thought there were too many Jewish people. He wanted to get rid of every newborn baby boy. One woman, named Yokheved, wanted her baby to stay safe, so she made a basket and floated her baby in the Nile River. She sent her daughter, Miriam, to make sure the baby was safe. The Pharaoh's daughter Batya was bathing in the river and heard the baby crying. She took the baby out of the water and named him Moshe (Moses, meaning "taken from the water"). Miriam said she could get a nursemaid (Yokheved) for the baby, so the princess kept the baby and he grew up in the palace.

When Moshe was a young adult, he went for a walk and saw an Egyptian taskmaster hitting a Hebrew slave. Moshe got angry and hit the taskmaster and killed him. Moshe was afraid that Pharaoh would be angry, so he ran away to Midian. There he met and married a woman named Tzipporah, and he became a shepherd. One day as he watched his sheep, he saw a bush on fire, but the leaves were not burning up. Stay tuned next time to see what happens!

Family Discussion Questions:

1. (Q) Who took the baby out of the Nile River? (A) The Pharaoh's daughter, the princess Batya.
2. (Q) What was the baby named? (A) Moshe, meaning "taken from the water."
3. (Q) Why did Moshe run away from Egypt? (A) Because he hurt an Egyptian taskmaster and was afraid.
4. (Q) Who do you think will speak from the burning bush?

VA-ERA

Last week we learned how cruel the Pharaoh was to the Hebrew slaves. Moshe was born and his mother Yokheved put him in a basket in the Nile River to save him from being drowned. The princess Batya found him and raised him as her son.

This week, in the parashah Va-Era, which means "and he appeared." Moshe saw a bush that was on fire but the leaves weren't burnt. It was a miraculous sight! Then Moshe heard a voice that said, "Moshe, take off your shoes, for this is holy ground." God told Moshe to return to Egypt (*Mitzrayim*) to ask Pharaoh to set the Jewish people free.

SONG: written by Emily Freedman, recorded by Jill Moskowitz from the CD *Miracles*

Moses was a shepherd watching his sheep, (3x)
When he heard a voice that said:
"Moses, Moses take off your shoes (3x)
For this is holy ground."
A bush was burning unconsumed, (3x)
And from it a voice said:
"Moses, Moses you must go back, (3x)
And set My people free."
Moses, Moses stand up and lead. (3x)
For your people must be free.

Moshe replied, "I can't do it! I'm not a good speaker."

"Don't worry, your brother Aharon [Aaron] will come with you and help speak for you," said God.

So Moshe and Aharon went back to Egypt to see Pharaoh. They went to the palace and spoke to Pharaoh, saying, "Let My people go!"

SONG: by Shirley R. Cohen

Oh listen, oh listen, oh listen King Pharaoh.
Oh listen, oh listen please let my people go.
They want to go away, they work so hard all day.
King Pharaoh, King Pharaoh what do you say?

"No, no, no, I will not let them go!" (2x)

After Pharaoh said no, Moshe warned Pharaoh that God would send Ten Plagues to Egypt if he did not obey. Of course, Pharaoh didn't listen, so God turned all the water into blood (*dam*). How will the people live without water?

Pharaoh said, "Okay, I'll let your people go. Just give us back our water!" But when the blood turned back to water, Pharaoh changed his mind.

So then God sent more plagues to Egypt, each time Pharaoh said they could go, but each time he changed his mind and would not let the Hebrew slaves go.

After the plague of blood, there were frogs (*tz'farde'a*)

SONG: by Shirley R. Cohen

One morning when Pharaoh woke in his bed
There were frogs in his bed and frogs on his head
Frogs on his nose and frogs on his toes
Frogs here, frogs there, frogs were jumping everywhere.

Then there were lice (*kinim*) everywhere, on the people and on the animals, and everybody was itching and scratching.

SONG (tune: "Skip to My Lou"—traditional)

Scratch, scratch, scratch your rosh (head) (3x)
Scratch the *kinim* away.

(Continue the song filling in all the different body parts in Hebrew or in English.)

Next, there were wild beasts (*arov*) all over the land that would attack anyone who dared to go outside. Only the Jewish people were safe from the plagues. Then God brought cattle disease (*dever*). The animals and cattle of all the Egyptians were sick and dying. Next, boils (*sh'khin*) grew on the skin of all the Egyptians. They were ugly sores that hurt and grew over their whole bodies. Then fiery hail (*barad*) fell from the sky, balls of ice and fire. They crushed the trees and plants and hurt the people.

Seven plagues so far and still Pharaoh would not let the Jewish people go.

MULTIMEDIA IDEAS

"ASK ME" STICKER: Ask me what punishments God sent to Pharaoh and the Egyptians.

MATH: Using counting bears or frogs or other animals, make groups of ten for the ten plagues. Can you make patterns using the animals too?

SCIENCE: Make red "goop" by mixing white school glue (like Elmer's), red food coloring, and liquid starch (two parts glue to one part starch) and pretend that it's blood. This can be messy! Wear smocks. If it's too sticky, add more starch—keep away from rugs.

COOKING: Make fiery hail by taking an ice-cube tray and adding a little clear soda (like Sprite), putting in a red candy (like Gushers or a piece of Twizzler), and filling the tray with more clear soda. (Optional: add a craft stick if you like.) Don't fill too full; soda expands as it freezes. Freeze and enjoy your fiery hail!

CRAFT: 1) Make a cooperative mural of the ten plagues using a variety of art media.

2) Make frog puppets from paper plates, folded in half, painted green to dramatize the frog song. After it's dry, add googly eyes or pom-pom eyes and a party blower for the tongue.

MOVEMENT: (inspired by Diane Holsten) To pretend to experience the plagues and leaving Egypt, set up an obstacle course that the children can go through. It is a good way to evaluate large motor skills. Have the children carry blocks (either cardboard or wood) from one place to another to signify the slaves moving the bricks; jump like frogs (like the second plague); slither like snakes under the table (like Moshe's staff); crawl like bugs; have the children straddle a red towel or cloth to signify the Nile River filled with blood to cross the river, etc.

Parashat Va-Era Family Discussion

(from *Morah, Morah, Teach Me Torah*)

In this week's parashah we find out what happened with the burning bush. God spoke to Moshe and told him to take off his shoes because the ground he walked upon was holy. God instructed Moshe to return to Egypt and to set the Jewish people free.

God sent plagues to persuade Pharaoh to free the Hebrews. The plagues were blood, frogs, lice, wild beasts, cattle disease, boils, and fiery hail. There were seven plagues so far. But Pharaoh's heart remained hard. ☹

Family Discussion Questions:

1. (Q) Who spoke from the burning bush? (A) God.
2. (Q) How many plagues did we read about in this parashah? (A) Seven. (Q) Can you name any of them? (A) Blood, frogs, lice, wild beasts, cattle disease, boils, and fiery hail.
3. (Q) Why were the plagues sent? (A) Because Pharaoh would not let the people go free.
4. (Q) What holiday is this story about? (A) Pesah/Passover.

BO

In last week's parashah, we read about some of the horrible plaques that were sent upon the Egyptians. God had sent seven plagues so far to Egypt (*Mitzrayim*), but Pharaoh still wouldn't free the Jewish slaves.

In parashat Bo we learn about the last three plagues. *Bo* means "come", and we see more plagues "come" to Egypt. The next plague God sent was millions of locusts (*arbeh*) that flew everywhere and ate the plants. But still Pharaoh wouldn't let the people go. God made the sky become dark (*h̲oshekh*). There was no light, and the people couldn't see. It was dark for three days! Still Pharaoh remained firm.

(See the song "March of the Ten Plagues" in Multimedia Ideas)

Moshe went to see Pharaoh and warned him that the last plague would be the worst of all. Moshe begged Pharaoh to listen and to set the Jewish people free, but Pharaoh's heart remained hard.

God told Moshe and Aharon what the Jewish people needed to do to prepare for the tenth plague. God commanded that the people begin counting the months by following the cycle of the moon. (When a new crescent moon appears in the sky, we know it is a new month. A new month is called Rosh H̲odesh, meaning "head of the month." (Just like Rosh ha-Shanah means "head of the year.") Later we will learn the names of the months. (For more information on Rosh H̲odesh, see page 273.)

God also commands that each family have a special meal called a Seder. They were to have a roasted lamb, bitter herbs, and flat bread called matzah. (Do you know what holiday we are talking about? Of course, Pesah̲ [Passover!] Each family was told to paint around their door frames to protect their houses and stay inside their houses. Today we still mark our door frames with a mezuzah.

That evening, God sent the tenth plague (*makat b'khorot*), and every firstborn Egyptian son died. It was a very sad time for the Egyptians. All Egyptian firstborn sons died, including Pharaoh's son.

Finally, Pharaoh realized that he couldn't win and allowed the Jews to go free.

We know that Pharaoh has changed his mind a number of times already. Should we trust him this time?

Moshe instructed the people to quickly pack their belongings. There was no time for the bread to rise so the people carried the dough on their backs, and it baked in the hot sun.

SONG (tune: "Happy Wanderer—Val-de ri—Val-de-ra," by Antonia Ridge, with adaptations by the authors)

Oh here we go a wandering through the desert sand.
And as we go we love to sing with our matzah on our backs.

We're wandering, wandering, wandering
through the desert away from Pharaoh.
Wandering, wandering, our matzah on our backs.

There was no time for bread to rise when Pharaoh said to go.
And so we grabbed all our stuff and off we will go.

We're wandering, wandering, wandering through the desert,
Moshe leads us. Wandering, wandering, our matzah on our backs.

God commanded the Jewish people to celebrate Passover each year and to eat only unleavened bread (matzah) for seven days. They were instructed to teach this story to their children because of what God did for us when we left Egypt. We must remember all the miracles!

MULTIMEDIA IDEAS

"ASK ME" STICKER: Ask me what holiday this parashah is about.

SCIENCE/COOKING: Make matzah! Matzah should be made and baked within 18 minutes, so set your timer! Mix flour and water and mix, on a floured surface, roll out part of the dough into a circle. Next, poke it with a fork on both sides. Then bake it in an oven at 400 degrees for 3–5 minutes. You could enjoy your matzah with some haroset. Chop apples (and nuts if there are no allergies!) and mix with grape juice and cinnamon and sugar to taste. Yum!

CRAFT: Make masks/costumes of the ten plagues to act out the story at your Seder. For the darkness, take white paper and white crayons and draw a picture or write the word "dark." Paint over the paper with thin, watered-down black paint. You can make locusts from clothespins.

SONG: "March of the Ten Plagues" (tune: "The Ants Come Marching One by One"—traditional)

Ten plagues kept coming one by one—oy vey, oy vey (2x)
They really needed some water to drink
It turned to blood and that did stink

CHORUS: And the Pharaoh said that the Jews could go, then changed his mind and said: NO NO NO NO NO NO NO NO

Ten plagues kept coming one by one—oy vey, oy vey (2x)
Then frogs were jumping everywhere
In Pharaoh's bed and in his hair

CHORUS

Ten plagues kept coming one by one—oy vey, oy vey (2x)
There were lice that were crawling on their skin
Then soon the itching did begin

CHORUS

Ten plagues kept coming one by one—oye vay, oye vay (2)
There were beasts roaming 'round and their cattle were sick
The locusts ate their plants so quick

CHORUS

Ten plagues kept coming one by one—oy vey, oy vey (2x)
Fiery hail was falling down from the sky
And darkness loomed everywhere, my oh my

CHORUS

Ten plagues kept coming one by one—oy vey, oy vey (2x)
Boils on their bodies, they were alarmed
And Pharaoh's son was also harmed.

Soon the Pharaoh said to the Jews—just go
And get out of Egypt NOW!

DRAMATIC PLAY: Have a practice Seder complete with Seder plate, four cups of wine, matzah, etc. Discuss what goes on a Seder plate and why we use these items. Practice the Four Questions.

Why is this night different from all other nights?

On all other nights, we eat all kinds of cakes, cookies, and breads.

1) *Why on this night do we eat only matzah?*
2) *Why on this night do we eat bitter herbs?*
3) *Why on this night do we dip our foods in salt water?*
4) *Why on this night are we allowed to recline while we eat?*

SONG: "What's on a Seder Plate" by Lenny Solomon, from the CD *SR for Kids Party Time*

What's on the Seder plate check it out and celebrate
Hazeret and the *maror* they remind me just how hard we worked in slavery
What's on the Seder plate check it out and celebrate
I see the *haroset* it reminds me of the bricks we built before we were free
What's on the Seder plate check it out and celebrate
I see the *karpas* it reminds me that once we were slaves and now we are free
What's on the Seder plate check it out and celebrate
I see the *z'roah* it reminds me of the *korban pesah* we used to see
What's on the Seder plate check it out and celebrate
I see the *beitzah* it reminds me of the Temple that one day we'll see
What's on the Seder plate check it out and celebrate
Passover it's so great we'll sing this song day one through day eight. Ahhhh

SCIENCE/CRAFT: God commanded us to begin counting the months by following the cycle of the moon. Learn about the phases of the moon. See Rosh Hodesh chapter for more craft ideas.

MOVEMENT: Hop around the room like locusts, frogs, or wild beasts to music. Then stop the music (like freeze dance) and say: "Run! Pharaoh says the Jewish people can be free." "Wait, freeze! He changed his mind!"

Parashat Bo Family Discussion

(from *Morah, Morah, Teach Me Torah*)

Last week we learned the first seven plagues sent to Egypt. This week we will learn the last three plagues.

Through Moshe, God sent the plague of locust and then the plague of darkness, which lasted for three days. Still Pharaoh would not let the Hebrew slaves go free.

At this point, God asked that the Jewish people begin keeping count of the months by following the cycle of the moon (Rosh Hodesh—the new moon and a new month). They were also told to have a special meal (a Seder) with roasted lamb, bitter herbs and flat bread (matzah). Each family was told to paint around their doorframes and remain inside so that the last plague will "pass over" our homes.

Then the last and worst plague came; death of the firstborn son of every Egyptian family, including Pharaoh's own son.

Finally, Pharaoh allowed the Jews to go free. They packed quickly and didn't have time for their bread to rise. God commanded the Jewish people to remember all the miracles that were performed and to celebrate Pesah each year.

Family Discussion Questions:

1. (Q) During which holiday do we eat matzah and have a special meal? (A) Pesah/Passover.
2. (Q) How many plagues did God send all together? (A) Ten.
3. (Q) Can you name any of the plagues? (A) Blood, hint: ribit, ribit—frogs, lice, wild cattle, cattle disease, lice, boils, locust, darkness, and death of the firstborn son.

BESHALLAH

In last week's parashah, after God sent ten plagues, Pharaoh finally agreed to let the Jewish people go free. But Pharaoh changed his mind many times before; do we trust that he will let the slaves leave?

In parashat Beshallah (which means "when he sent forward"), the Children of Israel (Jewish people) have packed their belongings and have begun to travel forward away from Egypt. As they traveled, they came up to big sea, the Reed Sea (*Yam Suf*—some refer to it as the Red Sea). What will they do? As they were deciding what to do next, they heard a sound. It sounded like a thousand horses galloping fast!

"Oh no! It's Pharaoh's army coming after us!" yelled an old man, "What will we do?"

"Do not be afraid. God will help us!" instructed Moshe. God told Moshe what to do.

However the people were afraid. Only Nahshon of the tribe of Judah had faith and waded into the water first. What will happen?

(Take blue paper streamers or blue fabric and have the children pretend to be the Reed Sea. Have them face each other and wave the blue streamers. Then have Nahshon start wading in. When he gets to his chin, have the children open up the streamer sea

to allow the people to cross. Make sure Moshe lifts up his staff. See songs 1 and 2 below.)

Moshe lifted up the staff in his hand, and as he lifted the stick, a great wind blew from the east and the waters parted! It was truly a miracle! The Reed Sea divided, and the Jewish people crossed on dry land. On either side of them was a wall of water, with fish and sea animals swimming by.

But the Egyptian army was following closely behind. As they reached the sea, they also began to cross the dry land to get to the Jewish people. As the last person reached the other side, God instructed Moshe to close the waters. Moshe did as he was told, and the Egyptians were trapped; they couldn't get to the slaves. The Children of Israel (*B'nai Yisrael*) were safe!

SONG 1 (tune: "He Waded in the Water and He Got His Ankles Wet" or "John Brown's Body"—traditional, with adaptations by the authors)

He waded in the water and he got his ankles wet,
He waded in the water and he got his ankles wet,
He waded in the water and he got his ankles wet,
But he didn't get his (clap, clap) wet (clap) yet.

Chorus: We are crossing the Reed Sea,
We are crossing the Reed Sea,
We are crossing the Reed Sea as Nahshon leads the way.

(Repeat with knees, tush, chest)

SONG 2 (tune" "Dayenu"—Passover traditional)

Moses lifted up his staff so
We could walk across the Reed Sea
The Reed Sea parted
We walked on dry land
And now we're free

(Traditional chorus "Da da-yenu," etc.)

Pharaoh soon changed his mind and
Sent his soldiers to capture the Jews
The waters spilled back
The soldiers were stuck
Dayenu

(Chorus: repeat)

Miriam (Moshe's sister, who followed him in the River Nile when he was a baby, remember?) led the women in *Mi Khamokha* and dance, playing their timbrels (like a tambourine), to thank God for the great miracle.

SONG (tune traditional, additional lyrics by Jill Moskowitz, from the CD *Miracles*)

Avadim hayinu, hayinu attah b'nai horin, b'nai horin
Avadim hayinu, attah (clap, clap) *attah* (clap, clap) *b'nai horin*
Avadim hayinu, attah attah b'nai horin, b'nai horin.

Once we were slaves in Egypt, in Egypt.
Once we were slaves in Egypt, in Egypt.
We were slaves, we were slaves,
But now (clap, clap) but now (clap, clap) but now we're free.
We were slaves, we were slaves,
We were slaves in Egypt but now we're free!

As the Jews traveled in the desert, they began to complain.

"Oy, there is no water! What will we do?" yelled one person.

"No water? Oy, we were better off in Egypt! Moshe, did you bring us into the desert to die?" shouted another person.

Moshe heard the complaining and, with God's help, found the water for the people. It was bitter, so God instructed Moshe to put in a special kind of wood and the water became sweet tasting.

Each day (except on Shabbat) God sent special bread for the Children of Israel to eat called manna. Each morning, there was manna on the ground and God instructed Moshe and Aharon (Moshe's brother) to make sure people gathered only what they needed. Not too much! If someone took too much, the manna became full of worms and bugs. Yuck! On Friday they were allowed to collect two days worth—for Friday and Shabbat. Manna could taste like whatever you wanted it to taste like. What flavors would you choose? (I'd pick chocolate cake!)

SONG (tune: "If All the Raindrops Were Lemon Drops and Gumdrops"—traditional)

If all the raindrops were manna from Ha-Shem,
oh how yummy that would be.
Mine tastes like hallah, mine tastes like cake.
Yum, yum, yum-yum, yum, yum, yum-yum.
If all the raindrops were manna from Ha-Shem,
now we won't be hungry, so say Amen!

Once again, the Children of Israel complained about water. God told Moshe to hit a rock and it would bring them water. Moshe was so tired of listening to the people kvetch and complain, but he hit the rock and water came out. The Children of Israel now had plenty of water.

There is a midrash (a rabbinic story based on the Torah) that a miraculous well followed Miriam in the desert the rest of their journey so that the Jewish people always had water from then on.

MULTIMEDIA IDEAS

"ASK ME" STICKER: Ask me what happened if the people took too much manna.

SCIENCE: Get out the water table and put in a little water (just a couple of inches). Use straws and blow the water. Can you make the waters part like the Reed Sea?

COOKING: 1) Make bread (see the Bereshit chapter for a hallah recipe). Just like God gave the Children of Israel manna in the desert, we can make our own. Add chocolate chips, apples, raisins, or cinnamon and sugar for different flavors.

2) Make "sweet water" like Moshe made for the people in the desert. Squeeze the juice of two lemons, and add water (about 4 cups) and taste it. It is bitter! Now add sugar and a craft stick or chop stick as the "special wood" to make it sweet. Taste the water again—yum! Make a chart of who liked the bitter versus sweet.

CRAFT: Make some timbrels (tambourines) from plastic plates or pie plates, wire (pipe cleaners), and bells.

MOVEMENT: Take out some tambourines and dance like Miriam crossing the Reed Sea.

SONG 1 (tune: "Twinkle, Twinkle Little Star"—traditional)

God made the sky rain bread
Manna fell upon our head
Gather enough for me and you
But on Friday, gather two
On Shabbat, no manna fell
Shabbat Shalom, all was well

SONG 2 (tune: "Yom Rishon Avodah"—Israeli traditional; lyrics by Diane Holsten)

Yom Rishon, a handful of manna
Yom Sheini, a handful of manna
Yom Shlishi, a handful of manna
Manna from Ha-Shem.

Yom Revi'i, a handful of manna
Yom Hamishi, a handful of manna
Yom Shishi, double the manna
Manna from Ha-Shem

Yom Shabbat, there was no manna (3x)
No manna on Shabbat boom boom

Parashat Beshallah Family Discussion

(from *Morah, Morah, Teach Me Torah*)

Beshallah means "when he sent forward". The Jewish people are free and are leaving Egypt. They come upon a great water (the *Yam Suf*—Reed Sea). Just as they reach the water's edge, they see the Egyptians in the distance. A miracle happens and God causes the sea to open, and the people cross on dry land. As the Egyptians are about to cross, God closes the sea, and the people are safe. Then Miriam (Moshe's sister) and the women sing and play their timbrels in celebration.

Soon the people begin complaining, because there is no water. Moshe finds water for the people to drink, but it is bitter. God tells Moshe to place a special kind of wood into the water, and it becomes sweet. God makes special bread (manna) rain down every morning. The people are told to gather only enough for one day. On Friday a double portion falls and the people are instructed to collect two portions (one for Shabbat). Again the people complain there is no water, so God tells Moshe to hit a rock for water. There is a midrash (a story based on the Torah) that a miraculous well followed Miriam in the desert the rest of their journey so that the Jewish people always had water from then on.

Family Discussion Questions:

1. (Q) How did the people cross the *Yam Suf* (Reed Sea)? (A) God opened the waters for the people to cross on dry land.
2. (Q) How did the people celebrate the miracle? (A) Miriam and the women sang and played timbrels.
3. (Q) How did the people get food in the desert? (A) God made manna fall from the sky.
4. (Q) Did it fall every day? (A) Careful, it's a trick question! No, it didn't fall on Shabbat.

YITRO

In last week's parashah the Children of Israel crossed the Reed Sea to safety. They began their travels in the wilderness, and God sent the people special bread, called manna, to eat.

This week we read Parashat Yitro. Yitro is the Hebrew name for Jethro, who was the father-in-law of Moshe. Yitro heard all about the miracle at the Reed Sea. After traveling a long time, the Jewish people entered the desert of Sinai. God said to Moshe, "I will come to you and My people in a thick cloud. Be ready; warn the people not to climb the mountain or look at the mountain."

The shofar was blasted so the people would hear and pay attention. Moshe went up onto Mount Sinai (*Har Sinai* in Hebrew). There was lightning and thunder. The people wanted to hear what was being said. God said, "These are the laws that I command you today."

The people said, "All that God says, we will do!"

(If you'd like to act this out, have a white sheet [for the cloud], cut out some lightning bolts, and some tablets [two swimming kickboards work great!], plus a costume for Moshe. Have some children be the lightning and some be *B'nai Yisrael.* Explain that our sages say that all Jewish souls were at Sinai, even those who weren't born yet. Hey! I saw you at Sinai! ☺)

In the synagogue, when the Ten Commandments are read, we all stand up because these laws are so important to us.

THE TEN COMMANDMENTS

1. **I am the Eternal your God** Who took you out of Egypt and out of slavery. **There is only one God.**
2. **You shall not pray to idols.**
3. **You shall not use God's name with disrespect.** Don't use God's name to swear or say bad words.
4. **Remember the Shabbat and keep it holy.** Shabbat is a day to rest, pray, and listen to the lessons of the Torah.
5. **Honor your father and your mother.**
6. **You shall not hurt (murder) anyone.**
7. **Married people should love each other.** (Do not commit adultery.)
8. **Do not steal.** Do not take another person's things without asking.
9. **You shall not tell lies.**
10. **Do not want what you don't have.** We should not be jealous of what others have. Be grateful for what you have.

MULTIMEDIA IDEAS

"ASK ME" STICKER: Ask me what special gift we got on Mount Sinai.

SONGS: Three songs

SONG 1) (tune "Ten Little Indians"—traditional)

1 2 3 4 5 Commandments
6 7 8 9 10 Commandments
Moshe gave us the Ten Commandments
Ten good rules to live by.

I am the Lord, I'm God
You should pray to only God
Do not say God's name rudely
And keep Shabbat each week

Love your mother and your father
You shall not hurt anybody
Married people should love one another
And you may not steal

Do not tell us any lies
Be happy with the things you have
Moshe told us ten good rules
They are the Ten Commandments

(Repeat chorus)

SONG 2) (tune: "The Bear Went Over the Mountain" or "For He's a Jolly Good Fellow"—traditional)

Moshe climbed up Har Sinai (3x)
To see what he could see

He saw the Ten Commandments (3x)
They were to be our laws

Moshe climbed down Har Sinai (3x)
And what do you think he did?

He read us ten good rules (3x)
And that's what Moshe did

SONG 3) "Ten Commandments" by Lenny Solomon, from the CD *Shlock Rock for Kids Party Time*

When Moses came down with the tablets
That is the *Sh'nei luhot* (two Tablets)
That was the Ten Commandments
The *Aseret ha-Dibrot* (Ten Commandments)

Now we'll teach you about the Commandments
In this little song
So here's a little melody
And you can sing along

There is one God, don't pray to Idols
Use God's name respectfully
Remember Shabbat and keep it holy
Your Mother and Father treat very nicely
The last five Commandments
Are how to treat all of your friends
So be the best that you can be
Again and again

CRAFT: Cut out the shape of the two tablets (*luhot*), and have the children dictate the Ten Commandments (or glue on a copy of the real ones). Practice writing *alef* through *yud* (1–10) in Hebrew.

LANGUAGE: Discuss and write down some good rules to follow in the classroom.

MATH: Name all the things you can think of that have ten: ten fingers, ten toes, ten plagues, ten pennies make a dime. Also you can group items in groups of ten and practice counting.

COOKING: Make a *Har Sinai* cake using a cake mix and baking it in a Pyrex bowl (sprayed with cooking spray) to make a mountain shape. Frost with green frosting and decorate with candy flowers. You can use graham crackers for the *luhot* (tablets).

BOOKS: *The Ten Commandments for Jewish Children* by Miriam Nerlove
Ten Good Rules by Susan Remick Topek

Parashat Yitro Family Discussion

(from *Morah, Morah, Teach Me Torah*)

Last week the Children of Israel crossed the sea to freedom. This week the Jewish people were wandering for a long time and enter the desert of Sinai. God comes to Moshe in a thick cloud on Mount Sinai (*Har Sinai*) and tells Moshe how to prepare the Jewish people to receive the Ten Commandments. The shofar is blasted, there's thunder and lightening and God says, "These are the laws that I command to you today." The people respond, "All that God says, we will do!" Even before they hear the commandments! Wow! What faith!

The Ten Commandments:

1) There is one God.
2) Do not pray to idols.
3) Do not use God's name disrespectfully.
4) Remember Shabbat and keep it holy.
5) Honor your parents (my favorite!).
6) Do not hurt (murder) anybody.
7) Married people should love each other (no adultery).
8) Do not steal.
9) Do not tell lies.
10) Be happy with what you have (do not covet).

Family Discussion Questions:

1. (Q) Why do you think they blew the shofar before God spoke?
2. (Q) Which commandment is your favorite? Why?
3. (Q) Do we still follow these commandment today?

MISHPATIM

Last week we learned the Ten Commandments. These are very important rules we still follow today.

In this week's parashah, Mishpatim, we learn about rules for making us responsible for our actions. If we promise to follow all of God's rules and remain loyal, then God promises to watch over us and keep us safe from our enemies.

God teaches the Children of Israel (*B'nai Yisrael*) to treat people who work for them fairly. They can only have a slave for six years and then they have to set him free. After all, the Children of Israel surely know what it's like to be a slave. They were slaves in Egypt for four hundred years!

God also teaches the people the rules if you hurt someone, even if it is by mistake. You must pay for the damages you caused.

If you lend someone money who is poor, you must be kind and not collect interest. If you borrow something, you must remember to return it or replace it (see Multimedia Ideas). Also do not speak unkind words (*lashon ha-ra*) about other people, even if they are true.

Remember to celebrate Pesah (Passover), Sukkot, and Shavuot and to eat only kosher foods.

SONG (tune: "She'll be Comin' 'Round the Mountain"—traditional)

Be responsible for your actions every day, every day (2x)
Remember God's rules, remember God's rules
Be responsible for your actions every day, every day!

Always treat people fairly, every day, every day
If you borrow something, return it right away
Don't try to hurt others, and remember to keep kosher
Remember God's rules every day, every day!

"If you follow all these rules then God will protect us," said Moshe.

Then Moshe (with Yehoshua/Joshua) went back up on Mount Sinai (*Har Sinai*) for forty days and forty nights.

Moshe tells the people before he leaves, "Aharon is here with you, if you need help."

MULTIMEDIA IDEAS

"ASK ME" STICKER: Ask me about ways that I can be responsible for what I do.

LANGUAGE: Talk about what it means to be responsible. (Examples: treating people kindly and fairly, honoring your parents by listening to them—cleaning up after yourself so no one trips on your toys and gets hurt, etc.)

DRAMA: Before you read the parashah story, drop various items around the room such as a wallet, a ring, a hair band, a bracelet, a mitten, a watch, etc. See if the children find them and return the "lost items" to you. When they do, say, "Thank you so much for doing the mitzvah of returning lost things (*hashovat aveidah*). That was so kind of you!" If they do not take your cue, then say, "Oh my goodness, I lost my wallet. Has anyone seen it?" See the song "Hashovas Aveidah" below.

SONG "Kibud Av V'ame" by Shlock Rock (tune: "Down By the Bay")

Kibud av v'ame, is what we do,
we listen to *Ima* and *Aba* too,
Clean up our room, so *Ima* will say,
Another mitzvah from our *Bnai Torah*, *kibud av v'ame*.
Kibud av v'ame, is what we do,
we listen to *Ima* and *Aba* too,
We do our best so *Aba* will say,
She's out of this world our mitzvah girl *kibud av v'ame*.

Kibud av v'ame is what we do,
we listen to *Ima* and *Aba* too,
No matter how old or big and tall,
We honor our Mother and Father too, *kibud av v'ame*

Kibud av v'ame is what we do,
we listen to *Ima* and *Aba* too,

This mitzvah is for every one,
We honor our Mother and Father too, *kibud av v'ame.*
Kibud av v'ame.

SONG (tune: "Down on Grandpa's Farm"—traditional)

Chorus: We're gonna eat, we're gonna eat,
gonna eat some kosher food. (2x)

Vegetables and fruits are all kosher. (2x)
Cows and chickens we can eat (Yum, yum!)
Ducks and goats and sheep (Yum, yum!)

Chorus

Please do not mix meat with milk (2x)
We should not eat cheeseburgers (Yuck, yuck!)
We should not eat pigs (Yuck, yuck!)

Chorus

DRAMATIC PLAY: Set up a library. Allow the children to "be responsible" for checking out books and for returning them. Another activity you could do is to figure out if anything in your school/house is borrowed and needs to be returned. That's the mitzvah of *hashovat aveidah*—returning lost things. Go through the Lost and Found at school.

SONG: "Hashovas Aveidah" by Uncle Moishe, Volume 3

Hashovas Aveidah, this is what it means,
Hashovas Aveidah, means returning those lost things.
Hashovas Aveidah, don't just turn away,
Hashovas Aveidah, means return them right away.

MATH: More age appropriate for four- and five-year-olds: Try counting to forty. Moshe was on *Har Sinai* for forty days. That's a long time! Make groups of tens to show that four groups of ten is equal to forty.

CRAFT: Make a coupon book out of paper with pictures of jobs the children can do around the house, putting their laundry away, cleaning up their toys, dusting, setting the table, etc.

BOOK: *No Rules for Michael* by Sylvia A. Rouss

Mishpatim Family Discussion

(from *Morah, Morah, Teach Me Torah*)

Last week we heard the Ten Commandments. This week we learn some other laws so we can live together peacefully. These laws are to help make us responsible for our actions.

We must always treat people fairly. If we hurt someone, even if it is by mistake, we must say we're sorry and pay for any damages we've caused.

If we lend money, we must be kind and not charge interest. We must always return what is not ours (either borrowed or found).

We must always speak kindly to others (not speak *lashon ha-ra*).

We must always remember to celebrate Pesah, Sukkot, and Shavuot and to eat only kosher foods.

If we follow these laws, then God will watch over us and protect us from our enemies.

Moshe and Yehoshua (Joshua) then go up *Har Sinai* (Mount Sinai) again and stay for forty days and nights. "Remember, Aharon is with you if you need help," Moshe tells the people before he leaves.

Family Discussions Questions:

1. (Q) Why are these laws so important?
2. (Q) How would people behave if we didn't have these laws?
3. (Q) Why is it important to return other people's things?
4. (Q) If someone borrowed a toy from you and did not return it, how would you feel?

TERUMAH

In last week's parashah we learned all about being kind and being responsible. This week we read Parashat Terumah, which means "an offering." God gave Moshe the plans to build the *Mishkan*. The *Mishkan* was a synagogue that the Children of Israel could take with them as they traveled. A traveling shul!

Moshe asked everyone to donate gifts to use to build the *Mishkan* and to give as much as their hearts told them to give.

SONG (tune: "B-I-N-G-O"—traditional)

God gave us lots of special gifts that we must share with others.
S-H-A-R-E (3x)
We share all that we have.

(Variation: Make the letters "S H A R E" out of paper to hold up for visual cues while singing the song.)

Some people gave many gifts like golden jewels, copper, furs and brass. Some people gave only a little cloth. People gave whatever they could give. Finally Moshe said, "Stop! You have been very kind, but we have plenty of things! Thank you!"

God instructed Moshe exactly how the *Mishkan* was to be built.

(If you want to act out this parashah, gather a few things to use as props to build your *Mishkan:* four poles or long blocks; gold paper to cover the wood; gold rings—shower curtain rings work well, or use paper and cut them out; fabric that is purple, blue, and red; two sets of wings and two halos—you can use large sheets of craft foam cut into wing shapes attached to elastic as wings and pipe cleaners formed into the shape of a halo; a small table; a gold seven-branched menorah; and some people.

This is a story chant to show you what they needed to build the Mishkan (as you mention each item have the children hold up the appropriate object):

Here is the Ark that Moshe built.

Here is the wood, two cubits long, that was used for the Ark that Moshe built.

Here is the gold, precious and pure, that lined the wood that was used for the Ark that Moshe built.

Here are the four rings of shiny gold that hung in the Ark that was lined with gold that covered the wood that was used for the Ark that Moshe built.

Here are the curtains, all purple, blue, and crimson, that hung on the gold rings that hung in the Ark that was lined with gold that covered the wood that was used for the Ark that Moshe built.

Here are the cherubim [angels] with wings spread wide that faced the curtains that were hung by gold rings that hung in the Ark that was lined with gold that covered the wood, that was used for the Ark that Moshe built.

Here is the *shulhan* [table] that stood near the cherubim that faced the curtains that were hung by gold rings that hung in the Ark that was lined with gold that covered the wood that was used for the Ark that Moshe built.

Here is the menorah, hammered in gold, that sat on the *shulhan*, that stood near the cherubim, that faced the curtains, that hung by gold rings, that hung in the Ark, that was lined with gold, that covered the wood, that was used for the Ark that Moshe built.

Here are the people who prayed at the Ark, that had a menorah, hammered in gold, that sat on the *shulhan*, that stood near the cherubim, that faced the curtains, that hung by gold rings, that hung in the Ark, that was lined with gold, that covered the wood, that was used for the Ark that Moshe built.

MULTIMEDIA IDEAS

"ASK ME" STICKER: Ask me what I would donate to help build the *Mishkan.*

LARGE MOTOR SKILLS: Build a *Mishkan* using blocks.

COOKING/*TZEDAKAH* PROJECT: Make brownies and donate them to a shelter or nursing home. Attach the following poem to the brownies:

We're sending you some kindness to brighten up your day.
We made some yummy treats to share with you today.

Fudge Brownies

1 cup pareve margarine
2 cups granulated sugar
2 teaspoons vanilla extract
4 eggs
3/4 cup Hershey's cocoa
1 cup all-purpose flour
1/2 teaspoon baking powder
1/4 teaspoon salt

1. Heat the oven to 350 degrees. Grease 8" x 8"-inch baking pan.
2. Place margarine in large microwave-safe bowl. Microwave until melted.
3. Stir in sugar and vanilla extract. Add eggs, one at a time (making sure to check for blood), beating well with a spoon after each addition.
4. Add cocoa; beat until well blended. Add flour, baking powder, and salt; beat well.
5. Pour batter into prepared pan. Bake 30 to 45 minutes depending on how fudgy you like them. Insert toothpick to test if they are done.
6. Cut into bars. Yum!

MATH: Using patterning shapes (rectangles, squares, triangles, etc.) build a *Mishkan* and count how many pieces you used to make it. Can you make a *Mishkan* using seven pieces?

LANGUAGE: God asked the Jewish people to donate items to help build the *Mishkan*, to give all that was in their hearts. Talk about what special things your children have made to give to other people. Why did they make things for others? How did they feel after they made something special for someone else? Make a language chart recording the children's responses.

CRAFT: 1) Look at pictures of the seven-branched menorah that is in front of the Knesset in Israel and make a cooperative mural of a seven-branched menorah. Use a variety of medium.

2) Build a *Mishkan* for your room from a box. This could be used in future parashiyot and for dramatic play too.

3) Create a weaving out of purple, red, and blue fabric or paper to represent the curtain over the Ark.

SONG (tune: "This Is the Way We Wash Our Hands"—traditional)

This is the way we build the *Mishkan*, build the *Mishkan*, build the *Mishkan*
This is the way we build the *Mishkan*, everyone all together.

Parashat Terumah Family Discussion

(from *Morah, Morah, Teach Me Torah*)

This week we read Parashat Terumah. God gives Moshe the plans to build the *Mishkan* which is like a synagogue that the people can take with them as they walk in the desert. It is where the Ten Commandments will be stored. Moshe asks everyone to bring gifts to help build the *Mishkan*, such as gold, silver and cloth, and to give "as much as their hearts tell them to give."

Family Discussion Questions:

1. (Q) Why was it important to have a *Mishkan*?
2. (Q) Why do you think Moshe asked everyone to give things to help build the *Mishkan* and to give "as much as their hearts tell them"?
3. (Q) Have you ever given something to help someone else and felt good about sharing?

TETZAVEH

In last week's parashah we learned about the plans to build the *Mishkan*.

This week's parashah is called Tetzaveh, which means "to instruct or command." God picked who would work inside the *Mishkan*, just like we have rabbis who work in our shuls. God chose Aharon, Moshe's brother, to be the *Kohein Gadol*, the head priest. Aharon was from the tribe of Levi and would serve in the *Mishkan* with his sons.

God instructed Aharon what special clothing the *Kohein Gadol* was to wear. Aharon and his son's were to be very special leaders, so they will have very special clothing, just like a king might wear a fancy robe and crown.

God was very specific about what should be worn: a special hat with a golden headband, pants, a long shirt, a belt, an apron (an ephod), and a breastplate that hung around his neck with twelve beautiful, precious stones to represent the twelve sons (tribes) of Israel (Yisrael/Ya'akov).

SONG (tune: "The Bear Went Over the Mountain"—traditional)

There are eight pieces of clothing, eight pieces of clothing,
eight pieces of clothing that a *Kohein gadol* wore.

There was a hat with a headband, some pants, a shirt, and an apron.
He wore a coat and a belt. That is what he wore.

There are eight pieces of clothing, eight pieces of clothing,
eight pieces of clothing that a *Kohein gadol* wore.

There was also a special breastplate, a beautiful, special breastplate;
there was a beautiful breastplate with twelve precious stones.

There are eight pieces of clothing, eight pieces of clothing,
eight pieces of clothing that a *Kohein Gadol* wore.

The *Kohein Gadol* also never wore shoes and had to wash and be very clean before he blessed the people. Even today, we have *Kohanim* who bless our congregations at special times during the year (Rosh ha-Shanah, Sukkot, Pesah and Shavuot), and they also take off their shoes and wash! Then they stand in front of the *Aron ha-Kodesh* (Ark) while the Ark is open, with their *tallit* over their heads. We aren't supposed to look directly at them as they pray. They place their hands in a special way. This priestly blessing is called *dukhenen*. In some congregations in Israel, *kohanim* (those people who descend from kohanim) give a priestly blessing every Shabbat! (See parashat Naso for more information.)

God also instructed Moshe and Aharon to have an always burning light in the *Mishkan*. The always burning light, or eternal flame, was called the *ner tamid* and it was lit with olive oil.

SONG (tune: "Bumping Up and Down in My Little Red Wagon"—traditional)

There's an always burning light in the *Mishkan*,
An always burning light in the *Mishkan*,
An always burning light in the *Mishkan*,
It's called the *ner tamid*.

Most shuls have a *ner tamid* even today, although they are usually electric now. Next time you go to synagogue take a look and see if you can find a *ner tamid*.

MULTIMEDIA IDEAS

"ASK ME" STICKER: Ask me about Aharon's special job and special clothing.

CRAFT: 1) Make a *ner tamid* for your own little *Mishkan*. Use a shoe box and cover it with pieces of tissue paper. Cover with a glue wash to make it shiny. After that dries, stick yellow, orange, and red tissue paper into the box so it looks like a flame.

2) Make an Aharon doll out of poster board. Then make all the different clothing that the *Kohein Gadol* wore, and make a paper doll. Go to www.Aish.com for coloring pages, too.

3) Make a breastplate for your dress-up corner. Also, talk about what the clothes the *Kohein Gadol* wore and what they looked like. Make a robe, an apron, and a headband to use in the family corner.

SCIENCE: Take a can of black olives and squeeze them to see if you can get olive oil like they used to light the *ner tamid.* A mortar and pestle works well.

DRAMATIC PLAY: Get out your dress-up clothes and play *Kohein gadol.* Make sure you have a few breastplates with twelve jewels on them! An old karate suit works great for the pants, jacket, and belt. You can use a Yemenite *kippah* and cut a headband out of gold poster board. Any apron and long shirt will work fine and you're ready to go! Try to dye the coat the colors that God likes (red, blue, and purple). You can use a pomegranate to make prints on the coat (God said there should be golden bells and pomegranates on the coat).

MATH: Discuss things that incorporate the number twelve (e.g. a dozen is twelve). Have egg cartons available to fill twelve stones, etc. Use English and Hebrew, of course!

COOKING: Make an edible breast plate to look like the one the *Kohein Gadol* wore: Take two squares of graham crackers, one above the other. Smear with cream cheese or frosting. Place twelve round pieces of fruit snacks, Trix or Fruit Loops of different colors on the crackers to represent the jewels of the twelve tribes. Attach a string of red licorice for the part that goes around the neck.

Parashat Tetzaveh Family Discussion

(from *Morah, Morah, Teach Me Torah*)

In parashat Tetzaveh we learn about the *Kohein Gadol* (the head priest) of the *Mishkan*. God picked Aharon (Moshe's brother) to be the person to take care of the *Mishkan* and to be the head priest. Aharon is from the tribe of Levi.

God tells Moshe exactly what the *Kohein Gadol* must wear. His clothing will be very special, just like a king wears a special robe and crown. Aharon will wear eight different pieces of clothing: a hat with a headband, pants, a shirt, a coat and belt, an apron (ephod), and a breastplate (like we hang on our Torahs today). The breastplate will have twelve precious stones on it to represent the twelve tribes of Yisrael (Ya'akov's twelve sons). We are told that the *Kohein Gadol* will bless the people (this blessing is still given in many congregations; it is called *dukhenen* [priestly blessing] and is done by descendents of the *kohanim* during certain holidays throughout the year). God also instructs that we have a *ner tamid* (an eternal flame) in the *Mishkan* (something most synagogues also still have today).

Family Discussion Questions:

1. (Q) Why do you think Aharon was chosen to be the *Kohein Gadol*?
2. (Q) How many pieces of clothing will Aharon wear? (A) Eight.
3. Why are there twelve stones on the breastplate? (A) For the twelve tribes of Yisrael.

KI TISSA

Last week we learned about the clothing the *ko'hanim* wore. This week's parashah is called Ki Tissa, which means "to take up a count of." God instructed Moshe to take up a count of how many Israelites there were. Moshe asked each person to pay half a shekel (that's what their money was called, as it is in Israel today) as a gift to God.

Moshe told his brother Aharon to take care of the people while he went up Mount Sinai. Moshe was gone a long, long time. The people were beginning to think that Moshe might never come back.

"Where can Moshe be? What has happened to him? Maybe animals ate him. Maybe God has taken Moshe from us," one person said.

"How do we even know there IS a God? We hear something. but we never see anything!"

"Right, we need something that we can see! Like the Egyptians—they had idols that they could see!"

"What are you all saying?" shouted Aharon. "The Egyptian idols couldn't do anything. I'll show you. This is what we'll do. Everyone, give me your gold jewelry, your rings, earrings, necklaces. Put them into this pot, and we will melt them down and build an idol that you can see. We will build a golden calf."

The men, except for the tribe of Levi, put all their gold into the pot and Aharon melted it down and built a golden calf. In Hebrew, "golden calf" is "*egel zahav*". The men were happy. They sang prayers of joy and danced around the golden calf. Then the men built an altar in front of the calf and had a feast. The women refused to participate!

God heard all the noise and looked down. "Moshe, look at what the people are doing! See how they have kept the commandments I gave them! You must go down and talk to them!"

Moshe carried the stone tablets—the Ten Commandments—and walked back down the mountain.

SONG (tune: "Johnny Works with One Hammer"—traditional)

He was walking down the mountain, the mountain, the mountain,
He was walking down the mountain and what do you think he did?

On the way down, Moshe heard singing, and then he saw what was happening. He saw the people praying and dancing and singing to a golden calf. When he got to the camp, he shouted to the people, "What do you think you're doing? You have made an idol! You are praying to a statue! Have you forgotten your promise to God?"

Then Moshe threw down the stone tablets, and they broke into many pieces. Then he threw the golden calf into the fire and melted it. The people stopped what they were doing. They were silent. They knew they had done something very wrong and they were afraid.

"We're so sorry, Moshe," they cried. "What can we do to make things right?"

That night Moshe called to God and asked God to forgive the Jewish people. God was angry. "What is the matter with them? They forgot an important rule to believe in only ME! They should be punished!"

"Please God, please give them another chance. I know what they did was wrong. I've spoken to them and they are sorry. Do you want people to say that You brought them into the desert only to let them die? Please, please forgive them!"

What do you think God did? God gave them a second chance. If they ever did anything like this again, God would have to punish them.

And so Moshe had to walk back up *Har Sinai* (Mount Sinai) once again. "I will be gone many days. Be patient and wait for me. Have faith in God. I will return, but you must obey the Ten Commandments!"

MULTIMEDIA IDEAS

"ASK ME" STICKER: Ask me what made Moshe so angry that he threw down the Ten Commandments.

MATH: Out of craft foam sheets (or poster board), make the shape of the Ten Commandments. Label it with 1–10 in Hebrew (א *alef* through י *yud*). Have the children cut it into a few pieces, making it into a puzzle (older children can make ten pieces) to represent the smashed Ten Commandments, and then have the children try to put them together.

LANGUAGE: Tell about a time when somebody made you angry, and write the ideas down. Discuss ways to resolve your angry feelings without being destructive or hurtful.

MATH/CRAFT: Take Israeli coins, and count and categorize them. Compare them to our coins. Make rubbings of the coins with crayons and paper.

SONG (Tune: "Bumping Up and Down in My Little Red Wagon"—traditional)

Where oh where oh where is Moshe (3x)
He's still up on Mount Sinai

The people have been waiting a long, long time (3x)
For Moshe to come down

Now they're tired of waiting for Moshe (3x)
They ask Aharon to lead them

Aharon tells them to build a golden calf (3x)
And that is what they pray to

When Moshe saw this he was angry (3x)
He smashed the Ten Commandments

We cannot pray to statues (3x)
There is only one God

Moshe begged for God to forgive them (3x)
Then he climbed back up Mount Sinai

Ki Tissa Family Discussion

(from *Morah, Morah, Teach Me Torah*)

The parashah we read this week is called Ki Tissa, which means ""to take up a count of." God instructed Moshe to take up a count of how many Israelites there are. God asked each person to pay half a shekel (that's their money) as an offering. Moshe had been up on Mount Sinai for a long time now, and some of the people began to doubt that there even is a God. They knew that the Egyptians pray to statues, idols they could see, so maybe they should do the same. The men all brought gold and they melted it down and built a golden calf that they danced and sang and prayed to. When Moshe came back down the mountain and saw what the people were doing, he was very angry, and he threw down the Ten Commandments and smashed them. God was angry that the people built an idol. Moshe apologized and begged God to forgive the people. Now Moshe must go back up Mount Sinai.

Family Discussions Questions:

1. (Q) Where did Moshe go for forty days? What was he doing there? (A) Mount Sinai, getting the Ten Commandments.
2. (Q) When Moshe came down from Mount Sinai, what did he see the people doing? (A) Praying to an idol!
3. (Q) How did Moshe feel about this? (A) He was mad!
4. (Q) What does Moshe do? (A) Smashed the tablets.
5. (Q) Have you ever been so angry that you wanted to destroy something?

VA-YAK'HEL

Before telling this story, have the children collect from the classroom a gift (e.g., play jewelry, animals, clothing) of some sort to use to act out this parashah.

In last week's parashah we read how the people worked together to build an idol. Let's see if they learned their lesson.

This week's parashah is called Va-Yak'hel, which means "and he gathered (the community)." It comes from the Hebrew word *kehillah*, which means "community" or "congregation". The Jewish people, together, helped to build the Mishkan. They were led by Aharon and Bezalel, the artist who was in charge of all the work that was done in the *Mishkan*. Everyone had their own special talent that they could use to contribute to building the *Mishkan*. For instance, some people were good at making sculptures, some were great at painting, some liked to sew things, and some were good writers.

In addition to the Ark (*Aron Kodesh*), the menorah, and the table (the *shulhan*), the people were instructed to make a washing station. Now the *Kohanim* would have a place to wash their hands and feet before they make gift offerings to God. Bezalel helped to build this as well.

SONG (tune: "This Is the Way We Wash Our Hands"—traditional)

This is the way we wash *yadayim*, wash *yadayim*, wash *yadayim*
This is the way we wash *yadayim*, *Al n'tilat yadayim*

Once on the right and once on the left (3x)
Al n'tilat yadayim

The people were reminded that on Shabbat no work was to be done. This was really when the rules of Shabbat were established: no building, no hammering, no cutting, no sewing. Any of the thirty-nine activities that were used to create the *Mishkan* would not be allowed on Shabbat.

SONG "The Melakhot," by Shlock Rock, from the CD *Woodshlock*

There's plowing and there's planting,
and there's harvesting and gathering.
There's threshing and there's winnowing,
and then there is selecting and there's grinding
and there's sifting, there is also kneading.
There is baking and there's shearing
and there also is bleaching.
There's combing, and there's dyeing
and plenty of spinning.
There is threading loom, and threading harness,
and there's also weaving.
Separating thread, there's tying and untying.
There's sewing and there's tearing
and you know there's also trapping.
There is slaughtering and skinning,
and there's tanning and there's smoothing.
There's marking, and cutting,
there's writing and erasing.
You must remember building
and you can't forget demolishing,
kindling, extinguishing, final blows and carrying.
These are the many tasks that were used to build the *Mishkan*,
they number thirty-nine and on the Sabbath are forbidden.

(This is when the children offer the gifts as you act out the parashah.)

Because the *Mishkan* was for the people, they wanted it to be really special, and they wantes to take pride in what they'd done. So, not only did everyone work hard to build it, but they brought gifts which would be used to decorate the *Mishkan*. In fact, they brought so many gifts that Moshe told them, "Your gifts have been appreciated, but we have enough gifts. We don't need any more."

MULTIMEDIA IDEAS

"ASK ME" STICKER: Ask me about what the Jewish people worked together as a community to build.

CRAFT: Organize a community project where the whole school or people in your neighborhood take part, such as a mitzvah quilt where everyone designs a square to add to the quilt. You might make it out of paper or fabric.

COMMUNITY PROJECTS: Make sandwiches to take to a homeless shelter. Are there other things you could work on together so everyone helps make a contribution?

MATH: Provide rulers and tape measures to measure things around the room. Using pattern shapes or pattern blocks, design and build your own *Mishkan.*

BLOCKS: Together, make a blueprint (using blue construction paper, chalk, and rulers) to build a *Mishkan* in your classroom or home, and then build it. This is a good time to set up a workbench and talk about tools and building. See what creations the children can design.

BOOK *Bone Button Borscht* by Aubrey Davis. This is a Jewish version of "Stone Soup" that involves a beggar taking a selfish town and changing it to create a community.

WATER PLAY: This parashah talks about the washing of the hands. Take out the water table, have a hand-washing cup available, and practice the ritual hand washing (right three times, left three times). Learn the Hebrew blessing:

בָּרוּךְ אַתָּה יי אֱלֹהֵינוּ מֶלֶךְ הָעוֹלָם אֲשֶׁר קִדְּשָׁנוּ
בְּמִצְוֹתָיו וְצִוָּנוּ עַל נְטִילַת יָדָיִם.

Barukh Attah Adonai Eloheinu Melekh ha-Olam asher kid'shanu b'mitzvotav v'tzivanu al n'tilat yadayim.

CRAFT: Since we've learned about the artist, Bezalel, it's a good time to learn about different Jewish artists, like Chagall, Mark Rothko, Peter Max, Gary Rosenthal (sculptor), Agam, Anni Albers (a weaver), Mordechai Rosenstein (silk screen prints), and Ebgi or Shalom of

Safed (prints embossed with copper and gold—see below). Create artwork such as stained glass windows: Cut small pieces of colored tissue paper. With a permanent marker, draw a design on white paper. Using watered-down glue, paint over your design and place tissue paper pieces over the top. Paint over the tissue design with the glue to flatten the pieces and give the picture a glossy finish. It will look like a Chagall masterpiece.

Va-Yak'hel Family Discussion

(from *Morah, Morah, Teach Me Torah*)

This week's parashah is about community. In Hebrew the word "community" is kehillah, and *va-yak'hel* means "and he gathered the community." The community worked together to build the Mishkan (a traveling synagogue). An artist named Bezalel was hired to be in charge. All the people were asked to bring gifts to help create the *Mishkan*. The people were very generous with their gifts.

In addition to the ark, the menorah, and the table (the *shulhan*), the people were instructed to make a washing station. Now the *kohanim* would have a place to wash their hands and feet before they made gift offerings to God.

The rules for Shabbat were established at this time. All of the work that was done to build the *Mishkan*, had to stop to observe Shabbat (the thirty-nine *m'lakhot*—hammering, cutting, sewing, lighting a fire, extinguishing a fire, etc.). God reminded the people to celebrate Shabbat.

Family Discussion Questions:

1. (Q) What does *va-yak'hel* or *kehillah* mean? (A) Community.
   (Q) Why is it important to be a community?
2. (Q) Everyone has a special talent. What's something special that you can do?
3. (Q) Did the people work together to build something? (A) Yes, the *Mishkan*.
4. (Q) Did they also make something for the *kohanim*? (A) Yes, a hand washing station.

PEKUDEI

Last week we learned about working together as a community to build the *Mishkan*. This week's parashah, Pekudei, means "records," writing down all that has been accomplished. Usually Va-Yak'hel and Pekudei are read together (except when it is a Jewish leap year). Pekudei is the last parashah in the book of Shemot.

The Israelites were working hard to build the *Mishkan* and to keep the Ten Commandments. But sometimes it was hard to build the *Mishkan* the right way, and the walls kept falling down. With the help of Moshe and Aharon, they will be able to build a sturdy *Mishkan*.

SONG (tune: "Johnny Works With One Hammer"—traditional)

The people work with hammers, hammers, hammers
The people work with hammers to build their *Mishkan*

The wood kept falling down, down, down
The wood kept falling down, what will we do?

Moshe fixed the *Mishkan, Mishkan, Mishkan*
Moshe fixed the *Mishkan*, God was very glad

All the hard work the people had done to build the *Mishkan* was finally finished. The *Mishkan* was all set up and ready for the people to pray there. Moshe was pleased with the way it looked. He gathers all the people together. Aharon, the *Kohein Gadol*, comes forward. What do you think he will do? He puts on his special clothes for the very first time. There is a special prayer that we say when we do something for the first time, the *She'he'heyanu*. Let's all say the *She'he'heyanu* together:

בָּרוּךְ אַתָּה יי אֱלֹהֵינוּ מֶלֶךְ הָעוֹלָם שֶׁהֶחֱיָנוּ וְקִיְּמָנוּ וְהִגִּיעָנוּ לַזְּמַן הַזֶּה.

Barukh Attah Adonai Eloheinu Melekh ha-Olam she'he'heyanu, v'kiy'manu, v'hi'gi'anu la-z'man ha-zeh.

Blessed are You, God, Who has kept us alive, sustained us, and enabled us to reach this season.

Moshe brought the tablets of the Ten Commandments, and where do you think they should be placed? They were placed in the Ark. Then the beautiful curtains were hung in front.

To show that God would protect the people and the *Mishkan*, God promised to provide a cloud over the Mishkan during the day, and a pillar of fire at night, just like God did as the Jewish people traveled in the desert when they left Egypt.

Look how far the people of Israel have come all these years! God forgave Moshe for smashing the Ten Commandments. Moshe tells the people that they can continue their journey into the Promised Land, where they will live and raise their families. Now they will travel for forty years through the desert to get to the land of Canaan (Israel), and Aharon will lead them.

Let's all say: "*Hazak, hazak, v'nit-hazek.* Be strong, be strong, be strengthened."

SONG (tune: "Mary Had a Little Lamb"—traditional)

Hazak, hazak, v'nit-hazek, v'nit-hazek, v'nit-hazek.
Hazak, hazak, v'nit-hazek—be brave and be strong.

We read five books of the Torah, the Torah, the Torah.
We read five books of the Torah and then we say *hazak.*

Now we finished the book of Shemot, book of Shemot, book of Shemot.
Now we finished the book of Shemot and so we say *hazak.*

Hazak, hazak, v'nit-hazek, v'nit-hazek, v'nit-hazek.
Hazak, hazak, v'nit-hazek—be brave and be strong.

MULTIMEDIA IDEAS

"ASK ME" STICKER: Ask me what we say when we finish a book of the Torah.

SONG: **(Israeli traditional)**
H̲azak v'amatz, h̲azak v'amatz, h̲azak v'amatz, h̲azak (2x)
la la la la la...

LANGUAGE: Make a sequence picture story. Either collect pictures of events that took place in this book, or have children draw them. Have children put them in the correct order. Some ideas might be: pyramids in Egypt, Moshe and burning bush, plagues, Moshe in the basket, leaving Egypt carrying their bags on their backs, the Ten Commandments, building the *Mishkan*, etc. (This is when you could use the coloring pages from www.Aish.com.)

SCIENCE: God made a cloud to follow the *Mishkan* by day and a pillar of fire by night. Learn about clouds. Go outside and observe the clouds. Learn about fire, and talk about fire safety.

Pekudei Family Discussion

(from *Morah, Morah, Teach Me Torah*)

This week we read Parashat Pekudei. This is important because this is the last parashah in the second book of the Torah (Shemot). Remember, when we finish reading one of the five books of Torah, we say "*Hazak. hazak, v'nit-hazek* (be strong, and be strengthened)." In Pekudei, the *Mishkan* was almost finished. But the people had trouble finishing it; the walls kept falling down. So they asked Moshe and Aharon to help build a sturdy *Mishkan*. All their hard work was done, and they could pray in the *Mishkan* for the first time. There was a special blessing that we say when we do something for the first time or when something is new, called the *She'he'heyanu*. There are many times when we say this prayer, which include the first time you eat in a sukkah, the first night of Hanukkah, when you wear new clothing, etc. Moshe brings the Ten Commandments and places them in the Ark. Now the people can continue their journey to the land of Canaan (Israel).

Family Discussion Questions:

1. The people couldn't complete the *Mishkan* unless they worked together as a team, or community. They needed to ask for help. Is it okay to ask for help? Even moms and dads sometimes need to ask for help. When do you ask for help?
2. Finishing the *Mishkan* was a really big job. Have you ever finished a really big project? What was it?
3. Where are the Ten Commandments kept now? Where do we keep our laws today in our synagogues?

VA-YIKRA

Last week we read about the completion of the *Mishkan* and how the *Kohanim* wore their special clothing for the first time.

We are about to begin the third book of the Torah, called Va-Yikra. Va-Yikra (Leviticus in English) describes the rules that the Israelites are to follow. You will notice that there may be some repetitions of the rules, because they were so important for us to follow.

The first parashah of this book is also called Va-Yikra, which means "and he called." Parashat Va-Yikra is about the *Kohanim*, the priests. They were like our rabbis, or teachers; they taught the people all the laws that God wanted them to follow.

God teaches the people about worshiping in the *Mishkan*. Remember when the people brought gifts to the *Mishkan*? Now the people brought different kinds of gifts; they were gift offerings made to God. These are what we call "sacrifices." It's sort of like a barbeque because some of the sacrifices were animals that were cooked on the altar. (Have the children bring blocks and play-food and build an altar and pretend to make gift offerings.)

In this parashah, we learn that there were different sacrifices, or offerings, at different times of the day. One offering was in the form of a cooked bird or a cooked sheep, goat, or cow. In the afternoons, an offering was made using flour and oil that was cooked in a pan like bread. Other types of sacrifices were when people didn't follow God's commandments and needed to apologize for a wrongdoing (they had to do *t'shuvah*) and say, "I'm sorry," or when someone made a promise but didn't keep it. The sacrifices were offered on an altar and cooked as a gift to God, but we know God never wants us to waste (that's the mitzvah of *bal tash'hit*—not being wasteful!), so the food offered was used to feed the *Kohein Gadol* and his family.

Today we don't use these kinds of sacrifices of cooked things. But we still ask for forgiveness when we've done something wrong; we still do *t'shuvah*. Every year on Yom Kippur, we say "I'm sorry" and ask God's forgiveness. Today, instead of sacrifices, we talk directly to God and pray.

SONG (tune: "If You're Happy and You Know It"—traditional)

Say you're sorry to your friends, to your friends. (2x)
Always try to be kind, always keep your friends in mind.
Say you're sorry to your friends, to your friends.

Today we don't have a *Mishkan* or offer sacrifices. We can go to a synagogue to pray, and some people also pray in their home.

Today, the *Kohein Gadol* is like our rabbi. The rabbi is our leader and teacher. But there are still *kohanim* in our synagogues. These *kohanim* are descendants of Aharon. In some synagogues the *kohanim* say special prayers in front of the ark. That's called "duchenen", which we learned about in Parashat Tetzaveh (also see Parashat Naso).

MULTIMEDIA IDEAS

"ASK ME" STICKER: Ask me what I would give as a sacrifice to say thank you to God.

DRAMA: Using puppets or pictures of animals, learn the names of the different animals in Hebrew.

BUILDING: Make a *Mishkan* from a box, and put play animals inside.

LANGUAGE: The sacrifices, or gift offerings, were one of the ways the people thanked God. How do we thank God today? We pray. Make a list of reasons we say thank you to God (e.g., for food, feeling better after being sick, returning home safely from a trip). Learn the *brakhot* on different foods. Make a *brakhot* book.

SONG: "Everybody Say Amen" and "3 Times a Day" from the CD *Shlock Rock for Kids Party Time!*

BOOKS: 1) Read the chapter "Croak, Croak" in *Seven Animal Stories for Children* by Howard Bogot and Mary K. Bogot. Talk about different ways to pray.

2) Do the mitzvah of *bal tash'hit:* check out the book *Green Chagim* by Nechama Retting and Tobey Greenberg, and recycle your way through the Jewish holidays. There

are lots of ideas to make ritual objects for the holidays (www.Torah4kids.com).

COOKING: Make pizza, either individual ones or a group, cooperative project, or make flatbread to symbolize what the afternoon offering might have been.

SONG (tune: Adon Olam—traditional/repetitive version, with adaptations by the authors)

Oh there are five [shout out "five" and put out your hand]
books of the Torah
Oh there are five (five) books that we read
Oh there are five (five) books of the Torah
We read five books of Torah each and every year.

First is BERESHIT, then we read SHEMOT
And then we read the book of VA-YIKRA
Then comes BE-MIDBAR, and last is DEVARIM
And then we start all over and we read it again.

Oh there are five (five) books of the Torah
Oh there are five (five) books that we read
Oh there are five (five) books of the Torah
We read five books of Torah each and every year.

Va-Yikra Family Discussion

(from *Morah, Morah, Teach Me Torah*)

Parashat Va-Yikra is the first parashah in the third book of the Torah. The word *va-yikra* means "and he called." This week we learn about the responsibilities of the high priest (*Kohein gadol*) in the Mishkan. They had to offer sacrifices three times a day to God (just like we pray three times a day). The sacrifices were also made when someone needed to say sorry for doing something wrong or for breaking a promise. Today we don't have a *Mishkan* or make sacrifices; instead we pray to say thank you and to ask forgiveness when we have done something wrong or broken a promise. Our offerings to God are our words (prayers).

The sacrifices were offered on an altar and cooked as a gift to God, but we know God never wants us to waste (that's the mitzvah of *bal tash'hit*—not being wasteful!), so the food offered was used to feed the *Kohein Gadol* and his family.

Family Discussion Questions:

1. (Q) How many books of the Torah are there? (A) Five.
2. (Q) Which book did we start today? (A) The third—Va-Yikra or Leviticus.
3. (Q) What is a sacrifice? (A) A gift offering to God.
4. (Q) Do we still make gift offerings today? (A) No, now we pray to say I'm sorry and thank you to God.
5. (Q) For what can you say thank you to God?

TZAV

Last week we learned about gift offerings.

In parashat Tzav, we learn when to make the gift offerings to God. *Tzav* means "a command" or to follow a certain rule. There were certain types of offerings to give: to say "I'm sorry", or to say "thank you." God also wanted the Children of Israel to give gift offerings at certain times of the day: in the morning, in the afternoon, and in the evening. Many people still pray three times a day to continue this tradition. In the morning it is called *Shaharit*, in the afternoon it's called *Minhah*, and in the evening it's called *Ma'ariv*.

(Divide children into three groups: the Shaharit [morning—you could have a picture of the sun rising on the horizon] group, the *Minhah* [afternoon—a picture of a full sun)] group, and the *Ma'ariv* [evening—a picture of a moon and stars] group. As you sing the song, have the children stand up as you mention each group.)

SONG: Three Times a Day (tune: "Three Blind Mice" by Uncle Moishe, from the CD *36 Jewish Children's Songs, Volume 1*

Three times a day, Jewish people pray (2x)
Shaharit is the morning tune,
Minhah in the afternoon,
Ma'ariv by the light of the moon,
Three times a day, Jewish people pray.

We also learne (again) that God wanted an always burning flame to be in the *Mishkan*. The always burning flame was called the ner tamid (see the "Ner Tamid" song on page 120). Synagogues still have a ner tamid even today! Next time you are in shul, take a look over the Ark and see if you can see one.

God again reviewed all the laws for making a gift offering: what to use, when to do it, why to make an offering, and how to make an offering. Then Moshe helped Aharon and his sons (the *Kohanim*) put on their special clothing (see the song on page 119) and helped them get ready to make the gift offerings to God, just as God instructed.

God also told the people never to eat blood. This is why we kasher our meat with salt to remove all the blood and why we check our eggs before we bake to make sure there is no blood in the eggs. The people were also instructed not to eat meat from an animal that was killed by another animal.

MULTIMEDIA IDEAS

"ASK ME" STICKER: Ask me when God wants us to pray.

HOUSEKEEPING: Set up your own *Mishkan* in your room complete with a table, menorah, altar and *ner tamid*. (Of course, have your *Kohein gadol* clothing available!) Have foods available for the gift offerings (bread, matzah, chicken, meat, grains). Talk about why you are making an offering (to say thank you, I'm sorry, etc.)

LANGUAGE: Write a chart of the different things you do in the morning, in the afternoon, and in the evening/night.

SCIENCE: Back then, people told time by the sun. The sun rises in the east, in the afternoon the sun is up above and the sun sets in the west. Study the pattern of the sun. Make a sundial using a small piece of clay with a pencil jabbed into it and a piece of paper to mark on, to see how the shadow moves throughout the day.

SONG: "3 Times a Day" by Lenny Solomon, from the CD *Shlock Rock for Kids Party Time!*

Abraham prayed in the morning
He talked to God, He talked to God
He knew it was best for his journey
And then he went on his way

Isaac he prayed in the afternoon
He talked to God, He talked to God
He knew it was best for his journey
And then he went on his way

Chorus: Three times a day I talk to God, I talk to God
Three times a day and many times in between

Jacob he prayed in the evening
He talked to God, He talked to God
He knew it was best for his journey
And then he went on his way

King David also prayed at midnight
He talked to God, He talked to God
He knew it was best for his journey
And then he went on his way

Parashat Tzav Family Discussion

(from *Morah, Morah, Teach Me Torah*)

Last week's parashah was about why the Jewish people gave sacrifices (gift offerings) in the *Mishkan*. This week, in Parashat Tzav, Moshe instructs the people about **when** to give the offerings. Gift offerings were given once in the morning, once in the afternoon, and once in the evening. Today we don't make offerings in the form of sacrifices; instead we pray to say thank you and I'm sorry to God. Some people still follow the custom of praying three times a day, just as the *Kohein Gadol* made gift offerings three times a day. When we pray in the morning it is called *Shaharit*, in the afternoon it is called *Minhah*, and in the evening it is called *Ma'ariv*. We can also pray anytime we want to! God again instructs Moshe about all the laws for making the offering.

God then begins to instruct the Jewish people about the laws for keeping kosher (kashrut). We are instructed not to eat blood—that is why we check our eggs for blood before we bake and eat kosher meat that has been salted to remove all the blood.

Family Discussion Questions:

1. (Q) How many times a day do Jewish people pray? (A) Three times.
2. (Q) Why do we check our eggs before we bake? (A) To make sure they don't have any blood in them.
3. (Q) Do we make gift offerings to God today? (A) No, instead we pray, we offer our words to God.
4. (Q) Do you ever talk to God?

SHEMINI

In last week's parashah, we talked about gift offerings. Remember, God instructed people never to eat blood? This is one of the rules for keeping kosher.

This week we read Parashat Shemini, which means "eight," and we learn that on the eighth day Moshe and Aharon and his sons were called and told more rules. God also told them to bring a goat as a gift offering. God then taught them what kinds of foods are kosher and are acceptable to eat and not eat:

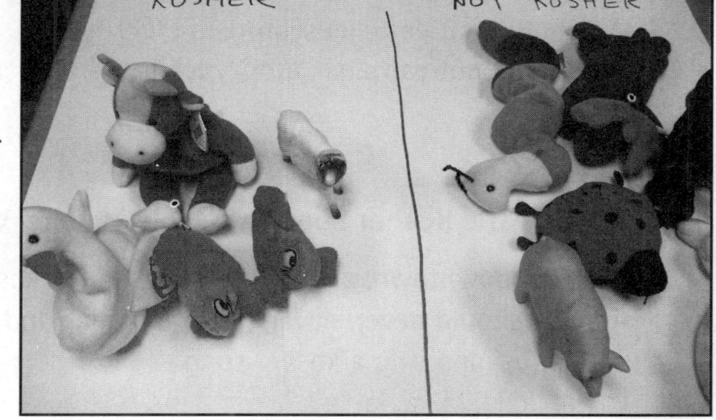

1. Fish must have **fins and scales.** Lobsters, shrimp, and crabs are not kosher, because they feed off the bottom of the ocean and don't have fins or scales.
2. Meat should come from **animals that have a split hoof and chew their cud** (they digest their food twice), like cows, sheep.
3. One rule of keeping kosher, which is told to us in the Torah is not to mix meat with milk. It says: **Do not to cook a kid (baby goat) in its mother's milk.** That is why today many people who keep kosher will not eat meat with milk products. For instance, they won't drink a glass of milk with a meat meal or put cheese on their hamburgers.

One of the ways we make foods kosher is by putting salt over the meat to remove the blood. One of the things that the *Kohanim*, our teachers, mentioned in this parashah was the importance of salt. Why is salt so important? When

God created the world, God created the oceans. The oceans that God created were salty. Salt comes from the sea and is used to make our meats kosher.

MULTIMEDIA IDEAS

"ASK ME" STICKER: Ask me about keeping kosher.

SONG (tune: "Down on Grandpa's Farm"—traditional)

Chorus: We're gonna eat, we're gonna eat,
gonna eat some kosher food. (2x)

Vegetables and fruits are all kosher. (2x)
Cows and chickens we can eat (Yum, yum!)
Ducks and goats and sheep (Yum, yum!)

Chorus

Please do not mix meat with milk (2x)
We should not eat cheeseburgers (Yuck, yuck!)
We should not eat pigs (Yuck, yuck!)

Chorus

SONG: "The Kosher Song" by Uncle Moishe, Volume 3

Uptown, downtown, all around the town it's kosher all day long
And we should never, never, never mix milk and meat together
So join us, and sing a kosher song
La, la, la, la, la, la, la, la...

BOOK: *Fins and Scales: A Kosher Tale* by Deborah Miller and Karen Ostrove.

SCIENCE: Try experiments using salt. Place an egg in a bowl of water. Does it sink or float? Now put a lot of salt into the bowl of water, and place the egg in the salt water and see if it will float. Try dissolving salt in water and see what happens. Can you still see the salt?

MATH/LANGUAGE: Have available an assortment of play animals, stuffed animals, or pictures of animals. Sort them in categories of kosher and non-kosher.

KOSHER	NON-KOSHER
cow	pigs
sheep	lobster
goat	crab
duck	cats
chickens	dogs
fish (with fins and scales)	rabbits
bison	octopus
moose.	squid
	shrimp.

SCAVENGER HUNT: Learn the different kosher symbols (*heckshers*). Look at food containers in the kitchen to find the different symbols (e.g., OU, OK, Kof K, Star K).

CRAFT: Collect the kosher symbols from food containers and make a matching game, a lotto game, or a collage.

Shemini Family Discussion

(from *Morah, Morah, Teach Me Torah*)

This week we read Parashat Shemini. God instructe the people never to eat blood and told us the rules for keeping kosher. Shemini means "eight"; on the eighth day Moshe and Aharon and his sons were called so these rules could be explained. The fish we eat should have fins and scales. The meat should come from animals that have a split hoof and chew their cud (that means they digest their food twice), like cows or sheep. We should not mix meat with milk (since a mother cow has a baby and creates milk to feed her baby, we should not cook the baby in the milk that was meant to keep the baby alive—it would be unkind.) One way we make meat kosher is by putting salt over the meat. A good book to read is called *Fins and Scales: A Kosher Tale* by Deborah Miller and Karen Ostrove.

Family Discussion Questions:

1. (Q) What does *shemini* mean? (A) Eight.
2. (Q) What do you do when you're cooking at school or home to make sure the eggs are kosher? (A) Crack them into a glass to make sure there is no blood.
3. (Q) How do we know which fish to eat? (A) They must have fins and scales.

TAZRIA

In last week's parashah we learned all about keeping kosher.

In this parashah, Tazria, which means "things that are not pure," we hear what would happen to people if they became sick with an illness that caused them to have "spots." The spots were called *tzara'at.* One of the jobs of the *Kohanim* was to check if someone had *tzara'at* spots. There could be spots on their skin, and the color of their hair would turn white. It could also get on their clothes as well. People had to stay away from the people with *tzara'at* until the spots went away. The people were separated from their community for seven days.

SONG (Tune: "Old MacDonald Had a Farm"—traditional)

Tazria, Tazria
Oy vey, OH!
Tazria, Tazria
Oy vey, OH!
With a spot-spot here and a spot-spot there
Here a spot, there a spot, everywhere a spot-spot
Tazria, Tazria
Oy vey, OH!

We also learn that the high priests, the *Kohanim*, had the responsibility of helping those people who were sick. Not only were the *Kohanim* our leaders and our teachers, but they were also like our doctors. They taught the people what to do about certain illnesses.

After the sick person was separated from the community for seven days, the *Kohanim* would check to make sure the spots were gone and the person was better.

There is a midrash (Rabbinic story) that says that people got *tzra'at* from speaking unkind words about other people. When someone says something unkind about another person, that is called speaking *lashon ha-ra. Lashon ha-ra* literally means having a "bad tongue." The person with *tzara'at* was separated from everyone else for seven days and needed to do *t'shuvah* (say "I'm sorry") before the *Kohanim* could check to see if they could return to the community.

> (**STORY**: Read *Yettele's Feathers* by Joan Rothenberg; a story about what happens to a woman who speaks unkind words about her neighbors. This is fun to act out as well. You will need a few costumes and a small feather pillow [felt glued in half and stuffed with feathers—make sure the top is not closed!].)

SONG (tune: "Three Blind Mice"—traditional)

Say kind words, say kind words
Don't speak *lashon ha-ra* (2x)
Always think about what you say,
Our words can hurt people, that's not okay
If you're wrong say sorry right away!
Say kind words, say kind words.

Did you ever have or did you know someone who had chicken pox? Chicken pox look sort of like *tzara'at*. But we know that we don't get chicken pox from speaking *lashon ha-ra*. Chicken pox are itchy, red, scabby sores all over your body, and you have to wait until they get better before you can go to school or play with friends. When we are sick or have an eye infection, we often have to stay at home, away from our friends until we get better. This is also what the people with *tzara'at* spots had to do—stay away from the rest of the community until they got better.

MULTIMEDIA IDEAS

"ASK ME" STICKER: Ask me about one of the jobs the *Kohein Gadol* did.

DRAMATIC PLAY: Set up your housekeeping center as a doctor's office, supplying it with lots of things you might find in a doctor's office (e.g., bandages, stethoscope).

MOVEMENT/GAME: Play "pin the spot on the person". Trace a child's body on poster board and hang it on the wall. Supply each child with a cutout spot (or circle stickers). Blindfold the child and try to put the spot on the child (i.e., pin the tail on the donkey game). This could also be used as an ongoing project to reinforce not speaking *lashon ha-ra.* Every time a child says something unkind, we say, "Oh no, I think we need to add a spot to our poster."

Tazria Family Discussion

(from *Morah, Morah, Teach Me Torah*)

In this week's Torah portion, we are learning about what happened to the Jewish people when they got sick. They developed spots on their clothing and bodies. These spots were called *tzara'at*.

The *Kohanim* were not only like our teachers, but they were the doctors, too. They were responsible to make sure the people with *tazara'at* (spots) were cared for and to check them to make sure they were clean after seven days.

There is a Rabbinic story that says that people got *tzara'at* from speaking unkind words, called *lashon ha-ra*. The person who spoke unkind words had to be separated from everyone for seven days, until they said "I'm sorry," did *t'shuvah*, and were clean from any spots (*tzara'at*).

We read the book *Yettele's Feathers*. It is a story about the town gossip (or yenta) who asks the rabbi for advice after everyone in the town will no longer talk to her. He advises her to take a pillow and cut off the top. After all the feathers go flying everywhere, the rabbi tells Yettele to gather all the feathers that flew away. The feathers were like her words, impossible to recapture and take back.

Family Discussion Questions:

1. (Q) What happened to the Jewish people if they got *tzara'at* spots? (A) They had to be separated from everyone for seven days.
2. (Q) What was the job of the *Kohanim*? (A) They were like our teachers and doctors.
3. (Q) What is *lashon ha-ra*? (A) Saying unkind words.
4. (Q) How does it feel when someone says something unkind about you?

METZORA

We learned last week all about *tzara'at* spots and about one of the jobs of the *Kohanim*. They were like our doctors.

This week's parashah is called Metzora, which means "the person who is not pure." Someone who is not pure is someone who is not holy. Based on midrash, (a Rabbinic story), someone who is not holy is someone who is speaking unkind words about others or gossiping. In Hebrew that is called *lashon hara*. Remember we talked about *tazra'at* last week? This parashah tells us what would happen if the person didn't learn their lesson and continued to speak unkind words about others. God told us to be nice to our friends and to be generous and kind to others.

(Choose children to come up and say either kind words or unkind words. Have the other children decide if it is kind or *lashon ha'ra*. See the Multimedia Ideas for other suggestions.)

In the days of the *Mishkan*, God would send "spots" to a person's clothes for not being kind. If that person didn't say "I'm sorry," or do *t'shuvah*, then God would send the spots to this person's body and it would make the person sick. Then that person would spend a "time-out" in a special place. The *Kohanim* would check to make sure the person was clean of spots and said "I'm sorry," and became pure again.

The person would have to give special gift offerings to the *Kohanim* to offer to God. These offerings were to say "I'm sorry."

According to midrash, if that person said unkind words again—uh oh, strike three, you're out! God would send spots to the person's whole house. Can you imagine icky stuff dripping from the walls of your house? Everyone could see that your house was sick and had spots. That person would have time-out again. But God always gives us another chance to do *t'shuvah* and say "I'm sorry." Hopefully this time the person would learn a lesson. And now the job of cleaning and fixing the house began. The *Kohanim* scraped off the icky stuff and plastered up the area. Then the person would have to give more gift offerings to God to say "I'm sorry."

Also in Metzora, we learn we should not be stingy. We should share what we have with others, especially when someone asks to borrow something. If your neighbor asks to borrow your tools, and you say ,"No I don't have any," even if you do, that's not right.

This parashah also talks about giving to people who don't have what you are blessed to have. Giving to others is called *tzedakah*. Sharing with others is the right thing to do.

(Now is a good opportunity to share your favorite *tzedakah* songs.)

MULTIMEDIA IDEAS

"ASK ME" STICKER: Ask me about how to share with others.

FINE MOTOR ACTIVITY/DRAMATIC PLAY: Get out the tools and do some fixing. Take out the sponges and spray bottles and help clean the *tzara'at* out of the classroom.

CRAFT: Have each child trace a hexagon shape, cut it out, and write the word "STOP" on it. Tape it to a stick. When they hear someone saying unkind words, they can hold up their STOP sign. The word "SHARE" can be written on the other side. This idea could be used during parashah time.

SCIENCE: Make goop (see the recipe on page 89), because the houses oozed with icky, sticky stuff (like the goop).

LANGUAGE: Talk about ways to use your words to SAY how you are feeling in a kind way (e.g. "I hate you!" versus "It makes me angry when you..."), and write down your ideas.

LANGUAGE: Teach the Hebrew words for words of kindness (*hesed*): excuse me (*s'lihah*), thank you (*todah rabbah*), please (*b'vakashah*), and quiet please (*sheket b'vakashah*).

SONG **"Selihah, Torah, B'vakashah," by Judy Caplan Ginsburgh from the CD *My Jewish World***

Selihah, todah, b'vakashah are words you should know.
Selihah, todah, b'vakashah you'll learn them as you grow.

Selihah means "I'm sorry."
It's a word that you should know.
Selihah means "I'm sorry."
You'll learn them as you grow.

Todah means "Thank you."
It's a word that you should know.
Todah means "Thank you."
You'll learn them as you grow.

B'vakashah means "Please."
It's a word that you should know.
B'vakashah means "Please."
You'll learn them as you grow.

Selihah, todah, b'vakashah (2x)

SONG **(tune: "B-I-N-G-O"—traditional)**

A good, kind person shares his toys
And helps his friends who need help
S-H-A-R-E (3x)
He shares the things he has

STORY: "A Happy Home" by Laura B. Tinter (see page 156).

A Happy Home

by Laura B. Tinter

There once was a family who did nothing but argue and complain. The father worked hard at his job all day and came home angry. The mother worked hard taking care of the home and didn't feel appreciated. The children were not grateful for what they had and said nothing nice to each other all day.

Every day it was the same. The mother would yell, the father would curse, the children would tease each other. It was not a happy home.

Even when the family sat down to dinner, it was no better—in fact it was worse. When they were all together the fighting just got louder.

"Meatloaf again?" the father complained.

"Well, if you don't like the food I make, you can cook dinner yourself!" the mother yelled back.

"You smell like a monkey!" the brother called to his sister.

"Yeah? Well, you look like one!" she answered.

It had gone on like this for years. One night, while they were sitting at the dinner table, their bickering was interrupted by the sound of dripping: drip, drip, drip. Water was coming from the roof of the house, and dripping right onto their dining room table!

"Oh great!" the father hollered. "Now I need to have the roof looked at. That's going to cost a pretty penny for someone to come and fix our roof."

"This house of ours is nothing but trouble!" the mother complained. "There is so much to do and so much to clean and then the roof has to start leaking? Everything is getting wet. Now I have more to do!"

"Yeah, and it smells in here," the daughter yelled.

"Like a monkey!" the brother teased.

But their complaining and yelling didn't solve anything, and the roof continued to leak: drip, drip, drip.

The next day, the family asked the town's roofer to come fix their roof. He climbed up on top of the house and went over every inch of their roof, but he could find nothing wrong. "Your roof is fine," the roofer told the family, "Maybe something is wrong with your plumbing."

So, that night they sat around the dinner table again listening to drip, drip, drip.

"Oh, GREAT!" the father said miserably. "Fixing the plumbing will cost even more than getting the roof fixed."

"And how will I clean the house or cook if the plumbing is broken?" the mother complained.

"How will I take a shower if the plumbing doesn't work?" the daughter asked.

"Yeah," the brother teased, "and when you don't take a shower, you start to smell like a monkey!"

The next day, the family asked the town's plumber to come and fix their pipes. He went through the house room by room, he checked every pipe and connection, but he could find nothing wrong. "Your pipes are fine," the plumber told the family, "You must have a leak in your roof."

So the family called in another roofer, and another plumber, and each one said the same thing, that they could find nothing wrong. The dripping got worse, and the family's fighting and arguing got worse too.

Finally, the rabbi of the town heard that this family was having problems with their home, so he stopped by for a visit. "You see, Rabbi," the mother said, looking tired and haggard from all her bucket emptying and floor mopping, "every roofer and every plumber we have brought in have said the same thing: there's nothing wrong. Well obviously there is something wrong because look at this place!" she screamed.

But the rabbi saw the problem right away, and he said, "I think I can help you. Invite me over for dinner tonight so I can talk to your family about it."

So, that night the rabbi came over and joined them around their table as they noisily complained and argued about whose day was worse. He listened as the children teased each other and the husband and wife didn't listen to what the other was saying. Finally, by the time dessert came around, the family noticed that the rabbi had not spoken the whole meal. "So you think you know what the problem is, Rabbi?" the father asked. "You know how we can fix our house?"

"Oh yes," the rabbi answered quietly, "I know what is wrong. Your house is not broken. It is sad. These drips are not a leak in your roof or bad pipes. They are tears. This house is crying."

"Oh *please*, you've got to be kidding!" the father sneered rudely.

"Not at all," the rabbi continued softly. "There is no love in this home. All day long all the house hears is arguing and complaining and teasing and yelling. It is sad for you, and it is crying."

"That's ridiculous!" the mother retorted.

Drip, drip, drip, responded the house.

"You may think so. But if you want your house to stop dripping, you have to start to show kindness to each other. You can begin now with each of you saying just one kind thing about the other," said the rabbi.

For once, there was silence in the home. The mother spoke up first, "Well, honey," she said to her husband, "you do work awfully hard to provide for our family. I do appreciate it," she said. Drip, drip, drip.

"And you work hard to keep it clean and have dinner ready each night. Oh, and you really do make the best matzah ball soup in town," the father responded. Drip, drip.

"I guess you don't smell too bad," the brother said to his sister, "for a monkey." Drip, drip.

"And I do think it is pretty cool that you can catch toads," the sister responded. "Can you teach me how to do that?" Drip.

And so it went. With each kind word the family said to each other, the easier they found it to say another. Pretty soon there was much less complaining and much more appreciating going on. Soon there was much less teasing and much more cooperating. The family began listening to each other instead of yelling at each other all the time. The brother even showed the sister how to catch toads, and she showed him how to pick up earth worms. The mother was whistling, the father was smiling, and the children were laughing.

The house had stopped dripping a while ago. Now, she was a happy home, quiet and content and filled with love.

Metzora Family Discussion

(from *Morah, Morah, Teach Me Torah*)

Last week we talked about *tzara'at* spots and about how the *Kohanim* served as doctors to help people who were sick.

This week's parashah is called Metzora, which means "someone who is not pure." According to midrash, if people still didn't learn their lesson about saying unkind words and they did it again, then this time their whole house would get spots. The *Kohanim* were called in again to clean up the houses and check everyone (including their houses and clothing) to make sure they were clean and pure again.

We also talked about the importance of sharing all that we have and the importance of giving *tzedakah*. It says in this week's parashah not to be stingy.

Family Discussion Questions:

1. (Q) What is *lashon ha-ra*? (A) Saying unkind words.
2. (Q) According to midrash, if people said unkind words again, what would happen? (A) Their whole house would get spots.
3. (Q) Who helped the people to clean up? (A) The *Kohanim.*
4. (Q) Is it important to give *tzedakah* and to share? (A) Yes.
5. (Q) Why do you think it is important to share?

AHAREI MOT

Last week we learned about how the *Kohanim* would clean people's houses after the houses became sick with *tzara'at*. We learned about being kind and sharing with others. We've also learned all about giving gift offerings to God to say I'm sorry.

This week's parashah is called Aharei Mot, which means "after the death of" (referring to Aharon's sons). In this parashah, God teaches the Jewish people about Yom Kippur. Do you remember in the fall when you learned about this holiday? Yom Kippur is a special day that comes every year at the same time. God said that on the tenth day of the seventh Hebrew month, all people must atone for their sins. Atonement means saying "I'm sorry" for the things we've done wrong (*t'shuvah*).

In parashat Bo we learned to start counting the months by watching the cycle of the moon. (See the Rosh Hodesh chapter for more information on the new moon.) The people would watch for no moon, and they would know the month was ending. When they saw a crescent or sliver moon appear in the sky, then they would know it was a new month. So that is how the people knew when the seventh month was. They didn't have calendars like we have today.

SONG: "There Are Twelve Months" by Lenny Solomon from the CD Shlock Rock for Kids, Volume 1 (tune: "Oh my darling Clementine")

There are twelve months, there are twelve months, there are twelve months in the year. (2x)

Tishrei, Heshvan, Kislev, Tevet, Sh'vat, Adar, and Nisan
Iyar, Sivan, Tammuz, Av, and Elul, now you're done.
In a leap year there are thirteen 'cause we added Adar Bet,
We can have such fun together, the Jewish year's really great.

There are twelve months, there are twelve months, there are twelve months in the year.

God instructed us to atone for our sins, to say "I'm sorry" for all the bad things we have done. God wanted the Jewish people to think about the ways that they were behaving and not to act like the Egyptians, who were praying to idols. God taught the people to say "I'm sorry" to anyone they had hurt.

God said that Yom Kippur would be like a special Shabbat because we must follow a lot of the same rules as on Shabbat: no working, no cutting, no hammering, no sewing. (Remember the thirty-nine things used to build the *Mishkan* that are forbidden on Shabbat? See Parashat Va-Yak'hel, page 127.

But Shabbat is a joyous holiday, and we celebrate it with lots of good food! God instructed that on Yom Kippur Jewish adults must fast—not eat or drink all day. If you are very young, or very old or sick, then taking care of yourself is more important, so you may eat, but you still should say "I'm sorry." God values life above all else! The people were also taught not to take a bath on Yom Kippur and not to wear leather. The *Kohein Gadol* had another set of special clothing for this day; it was all white. Some people today wear an all-white garment called a kittle on Yom Kippur.

To announce the end of Yom Kippur, after sundown, the shofar was blown. *T'kiah g'dolah*!

SONG (tune: "Twinkle, Twinkle"—traditional)

Yom Kippur is here at last
A *Yom Tov* day on which we fast
We go to shul and stay all day
We ask forgiveness when we pray
Yom Kippur is here at last
A *Yom Tov* day on which we fast.

If the Jewish people did not obey the laws, God said that they would be cut off from their people and cut off from their community. That would be so sad not to have any family or friends!

MULTIMEDIA IDEAS

"ASK ME" STICKER: Ask me what the *Kohein gadol* wore on Yom Kippur.

CRAFTS: 1) Make a "*middot* jar." *Middot* are good manners. Take a jar or container and decorate it. When you see someone using good *middot* (e.g., being kind, sharing), write down the kind thing or add a few coins to the jar. On Shabbat read all the kind things you wrote down during the week, or when it's full of coins, buy something special for your school or home, or have a party! (You could also make a classroom *middot* tree and add leaves or a classroom pomegranate/*rimon* (for seeds of good deeds) and add a [fingerprint] seed each time someone does something kind.)

2) Make a kittel out of a white pillowcase to add to your dress up corner. Cut out a neck hole and armholes, and then make a white belt.

3) Make a shofar out of poster board and add a party blower (the noisy kind!).

4) Make a calendar with the Hebrew months. Find out when everyone's Hebrew birthday is. Go to www.hebcal.com/converter.

STORY: Find and read the story *Jonah and the Whale.*

Aharei Mot Family Discussion

This week we learned about Yom Kippur and saying "I'm sorry." God instructed us to atone for our sins, to say "I'm sorry" for all the bad things we have done. God wanted the Jewish people to think about the ways they were behaving and not to act like the Egyptians, who prayed to idols. God taught them to say "I'm sorry" to anyone they had hurt.

God said that Yom Kippur should be a special holiday and we should follow the same as those we follow on Shabbat. But on Shabbat we eat festive meals' on Yom Kippur, adults fast and cannot eat or drink all day.

If you are very young, or very old or sick then taking care of yourself is more important, so you may eat, but you still should say "I'm sorry." God values life above all else! The people were also taught not to take a bath on Yom Kippur and not to wear leather. The *Kohein Gadol* had another set of special clothing for this day, it was pure white, like the kittel some people wear on Yom Kippur today.

To announce the end of Yom Kippur, after sundown, the shofar was blown. *T'kiah g'dolah*!

Family Discussion Questions:

1. (Q) What is Yom Kippur? (A) The holiday when we say "I'm sorry."
2. (Q) What do adults do on Yom Kippur? (A) Fast and pray.
3. (Q) Did the *Kohein Gadol* wear special clothing on Yom Kippur? (A) Yes, a white kittel.
4. (Q) How do we know that Yom Kippur is over? (A) The shofar blows.

KEDOSHIM

Last week we learned about one of the holiest days of the year, Yom Kippur.

This week's parashah is called Kedoshim. Kedoshim comes from the Hebrew word *kadosh*, which means "holy." What does it mean to be holy? Being holy can mean many different things. It can mean being unique or special, or being close to God. Remember in Bereshit, we learned that each of us was made in God's image (*b'tzelem Elohim*)? It's what makes YOU the person you are, what makes you different and unique from others. That's what makes YOU special.

SONG: "You Are So Special" (tune: "You Are My Sunshine" by Jimmie Davis and Charles Mitchell, with adaptations by the authors)

You are so special, so very special
You're the only one like you
You were created in God's image
No one else does the things that you do.

God tells Moshe "to be holy, for I (God) am holy" and to instruct the Israelites "not to put a stumbling block before the blind," "to love your neighbor as yourself," and not to insult or make fun of people who are not perfect or who are different from yourself. These words are part of our morning prayers said during *Shaharit*. You are to be kind to others. **Treat others the way you would like to be treated**. For instance, if you see someone who is blind, or deaf, or in a wheelchair or walks with a cane or crutches, you may not make fun of them, or laugh at them. They would want you to treat them just like you would treat anyone else.

(Allow the children the opportunity to see what it would be like to be disabled: earmuffs so they can't hear well, wear a blindfold to see what it's like to be blind and have a friend lead them, try to maneuver around in a wheelchair by themselves.

Love your neighbors and friends as you would love yourself (*ahavat Yisrael*). If you don't want your friends to tease you or to say you can't play with them, then you shouldn't tease them or tell them they can't play with you. Treat them the way you would like to be treated.

SONG (tune "Adon Olam"—traditional, the repetitive version)

Kadosh, kadosh
Means please be holy
Kadosh, kadosh
Treat others we-e-ell.
Kadosh, Kadosh
Try to be kind.
Treat your friends the way you want to be treated.

MULTIMEDIA IDEAS

"ASK ME" STICKER: Ask me what makes me special.

BOOKS: 1) *Moses Goes to a Concert* by Yitzchak Millman This is a story about a boy who is deaf, but still enjoys going to a concert.

2) *A Very Special Critter* by Gina and Mercer Mayer.

LANGUAGE/CRAFT: 1) Invite children to talk about what makes them special, what makes them the unique person they are. Write down their ideas, have them draw a picture, and make it into a book. Talk about being created in God's image.

2) Talk about Braille. Bring in a book from the library with Braille writing for the children to feel. Look for Braille writing on signs in your school or your community.

CRAFT: *Kedoshim, Kadosh* and *Kiddush* all come from the same Hebrew root word. Make a special Shabbat craft to help make your Shabbat table more holy (candles, candlesticks, kiddush cup, hallah cover, Shabbat flowers, or a vase to take home to put their Shabbat flowers into.)

Parashat Kedoshim Family Discussion

(from *Morah, Morah, Teach Me Torah*)

This week's parashah is about being holy (*kadosh*). God said, "Be holy, for I, the Eternal your God am holy." Being holy means that we are created in God's image and we are all special in our own way. It's is what makes us unique.

God also instructed us "not to put a stumbling block before the blind." That means that we should be kind to everyone, especially someone who is handicapped. We should love our neighbors as we love ourselves (*ahavat Yisrael*)—treat our friends the way we want to be treated.

Family Discussion Questions:

1. (Q) What does *kadosh* and *kedoshim* mean? (A) Holy.
2. (Q) What do you think it means to be created in God's image?
3. (Q) Would you laugh at a friend who got glasses or broke his or her arm?
4. (Q) What do you think it means to love your neighbor as yourself?

EMOR

In last week's parashah we learned all about being holy. This week's parashah is Emor, which means "to say." It comes from the Hebrew root word that means "to say." Moshe is instructed to speak to the people about all the holy days in the year. Besides Shabbat, which comes each week (every seven days), the Israelites are to observe the feast of unleavened bread. Who knows what holiday that is? (Pesah.) Then seven weeks later we rejoice with a celebration of the harvest. We even count the weeks until the holiday! Which holiday celebrates the harvest and comes after Pesah? (Shavuot.) On the first day of the seventh month of the year, the people are commanded to observe a holiday by sounding the shofar (Rosh ha-Shanah.) Next we observe the Day of Atonement, when we ask God to forgive us (Yom Kippur). Then we observe the Feast of Booths. The booth is called a sukkah, and the holiday is Sukkot, of course, which in Israel is observed for seven days.

On every holiday, the *Kohanim* have special jobs to do. They do their most important work on holidays.

(**GAME**: We are going to play a game like charades that acts out the different holidays. Each class will give us clues to a holiday by acting out things we know about that holiday, and the rest of us will try to guess which holiday it is. (Examples: Rosh ha-Shanah—shofar, apples, honey; Yom Kippur—wear your kittel, look sad and say "I'm sorry.")

MULTIMEDIA IDEAS

"ASK ME" STICKER: Ask me what my favorite Jewish holiday is.

BOOKS: *A Jewish Holiday ABC* by Malka Drucker and Rita Pocock.

Special Days Are Wonderful by Miriam L. Elias.

MATH: The number seven appears many times in this parashah. Count and sort objects into groups of seven. Using clay, form the number seven. Write the number seven on a piece of paper and have the children put seven stickers onto the paper.

SCIENCE: Since this parashah is usually read during the counting of the Omer (time between Pesah and Shavuot), try planting wheat or barley (one of the seven species) and harvest it next year. To purchase seeds, go to www.boldweb.com/greenweb.htm. They also sell carob seeds.

GAME: Play *Moshe Omare*—"Moses Says" (like "Simon Says").

SONG (tune: "Bumping Up and Down in My Little Red Wagon"—traditional)

When do we eat apples and honey? (3x) On Rosh Ha-Shanah.
When do we say "I'm sorry"? (3x) On Yom Kippur.
When do we shake a *lulav*? (3x) On the holiday of Sukkot.
When do we march with the Torahs? (3x) On Simhat Torah.
When do we spin a dreidel? (3x) On the holiday of Hanukkah.
When do we plant a tree? (3x) On the holiday of Tu B'Shevat.
When do we twirl our groggers? (3x) On the holiday of Purim.
When do we eat only matzah? (3x) On the holiday of Pesah.
When do we read the Ten Commandments? (3x)
On the holiday of Shavuot.

Parashat Emor Family Discussion

(from *Morah, Morah, Teach Me Torah*)

This week we read Parashat Emor, which means "to speak" or "to say." Moshe is instructed to speak to the people about all the holy days in the year. We know that Shabbat comes every seven days. We recently celebrated the holiday of unleavened bread (Pesah, which in Israel lasts for seven days). Seven weeks after Pesah, we celebrate a holiday of the harvest (Shavuot). On the first day of the seventh month of the Hebrew year, we listen to the sound of the shofar (Rosh ha-Shanah). Then comes Yom Kippur when we say "I'm sorry" for the things we did that we shouldn't have. Then we celebrate the festival of booths (Sukkot), which in Israel is also celebrated for seven days. On each of these holidays, the *Kohanim* have special jobs to do.

Family Discussion Questions:

1. (Q) What number keeps appearing in this parashah? (A) Seven.
2. (Q) There are more things with the number seven. Can you think of others? (A) The seven-branched menorah in Israel; the "seven species" that are so important to Israel—dates, figs, pomegranates, olives, wheat, barley, and grapes; the seven days of the week.
3. (Q) Which holidays have we celebrated at school so far this year? Do you remember them?

BE-HAR

Last week we tried to remember all the Jewish holidays. This week we continue our journey in the desert near *Har Sinai* (Mount Sinai) with the reading of Parashat Be-Har.

The word be-har means "on the mountain." Why do you think this mountain is so important? Mount Sinai is important because this is where God's laws were given to Moshe.

Moshe talks to the Israelites about more laws that they should follow when they enter the land that God promised them. Do you know what land that is? (Is it Egypt? No way!) It's the land of Canaan (now called Israel).

Moshe instructs the people that for six years they can plant and harvest crops—fruits and vegetables and grain from their fields and vineyards. But the seventh year they must let the land rest. In that seventh year, which is called *sh'mittah*, they cannot work in their fields or plant anything. But they can gather what they have, and they are allowed to share whatever the land produces with others. There will be enough food for the people even if they share with others who don't have any food. It is a Shabbat for the land.

(Have children put play vegetables and fruits all over the floor. Then have the children find them and share them with other children. You can repeat this as many times as you like.)

Let's sing some songs about sharing and *sh'mittah* (resting the land):

SONG (tune: "B-I-N-G-O"—traditional)

God gave us lots of special gifts that we must share with others
S-H-A-R-E (3x)
We share all that we have
God gave us the gift of Shabbat so we could share with others
S-H-A-R-E (3x)
We share all that we have.

SONG (tune: "Eency Weency Spider"—traditional)

Sh'mittah is the seventh year, Shabbat for the land
Six years we plant, the best that we can.
On the seventh year, we let the land rest,
Then we share all that we have
'Cause sharing is the best.

MULTIMEDIA IDEAS

"ASK ME" STICKER: Ask me about the Shabbat for the land.

MATH: Let's see how we can make groups of seven.

BOOK: *As Big As an Egg* by Rochel Sandman—a true story about sharing.

COOKING: Make fruit salad and/or vegetable salad to share.

LANGUAGE: We hear the number seven lots of times in Judaism. What can you think of that has the number seven in it?

1) Seven days of the week.
2) The seventh day of the week is Shabbat.
3) Seven branches of the menorah in front of the Knesset in Israel.
4) Seven days of Sukkot (in Israel).
5) Seven days of Pesah (in Israel).
6) Seven weeks of counting the Omer, from Pesah until Shavuot.
7) When a man and a woman get married, seven blessings (*sheva brakhot*) are said. Then the bride walks around the groom seven times.
8) During the seventh year there would be no planting.

Parashat Be-Har Family Discussion

(from *Morah, Morah, Teach Me Torah*)

This week's parashah is Be-Har, which means, "on the mountain." What mountain do you think we are talking about? *Har Sinai*, Mount Sinai. This mountain is so important because this is where Moshe receives the Ten Commandments. Moshe talks to the Israelites about more laws that the people should know when they enter the land of Canaan. Then Moshe instructs the people that for six years they should plant and harvest fruits and vegetables and grains to live on. Then during the seventh year, they should let the land rest. They can't plant anything, but they should share what they have with those who don't have food. This seventh year is called *sh'mittah*—the Shabbat of the land.

Family Discussion Questions:

1. (Q) *Be-har* means "on the mountain." Which mountain are they talking about? (A) Mount Sinai, *Har Sinai.*
2. (Q) We read about planting the crops for six years and letting the land rest during the seventh year, *sh'mittah*. What should the people do with their crops? (A) Share what they have with others.
3. (Q) We let the land rest on the seventh year. What do we do on the seventh day of the week? (A) Rest—it's Shabbat.
4. (Q) Can you name the days of the week and count them? Can you recite them in Hebrew?

BE-HUKKOTAI

Last week we learned about sharing and *sh'mittah*. We're almost finished reading Va-Yikra, the third book of the Torah.

This is the last parashah in the book of Va-Yikra. It's called Be-Hukkotai, which means "in My commandments." God has taught the Jewish people lots of laws. God promised *B'nai Yisrael* (the Jewish people) many blessings if they obeyed and followed all of the laws. They would have peace in their land, no enemies, lots of crops and food, plenty of rain, no wild beasts, and lots of children. These were like the plagues the Egyptians experienced. "I will stay with you, I will be your God, and you will be My people. Remember I brought you out of slavery in Egypt and set you free," said God.

SONG (tune: "You Are My Sunshine," by Jimmie Davis and Charles Mitchell, with adaptations by the authors)

God gave us
Lots of laws
They're the rules we should obey
If we follow
All the commandments
Then God will reward us all!

If we follow
All the rules
Then God will give to us
Rain for the land
And no enemies.
God will reward us all!

God then lists all the terrible things that will happen if the Jewish people don't follow the laws. The land will dry up, and no food will grow. They will be at war all the time. God will curse the people and not bless them any more. But, if they do *t'shuvah*, say "I'm sorry," then God will forgive them.

We learned so many laws and commandments in the book of Va-Yikra. Which commandment do you think is the most important?

Do you remember what we say at the end of a book of the Torah?

SONG (tune: Mary Had a Little Lamb—traditional)

Hazak, Hazak, v'nit-hazek, v'nit-hazek, v'nit-hazek.
Hazak, Hazak, v'nit-hazek—be brave and be strong.

We read five books of the Torah, the Torah, the Torah.
We read five books of the Torah and then we say *hazak.*

Now we finished Va-Yikra, Va-Yikra, Va-Yikra.
Now we finished Va-Yikra and so we say *hazak.*

Hazak, Hazak, v'nit-hazek, v'nit-hazek, v'nit-hazek.
Hazak, Hazak, v'nit-hazek—be brave and be strong.

MULTIMEDIA IDEAS

"ASK ME" STICKER: Ask me about what happens when I follow the rules (or don't follow the rules).

SCIENCE: God promised lots of crops to grow for the Jewish people. Plant seeds and watch them grow. (apple seeds, flowers, sprouts, parsley).

SCIENCE/LANGUAGE: After the plants have sprouted, do experiments to show how a plant reacts to rain versus no rain, and light versus no light. Chart your predictions, and after a couple of weeks chart your results.

CRAFT/LANGUAGE: Make a list of class rules (or house rules). Talk about the rules and consequences. List them on paper shaped like the tablets (*luhot*) of the Ten Commandments.

Parashat Be-Hukkotai Family Discussion

(from *Morah, Morah, Teach Me Torah*)

This week's parashah is Be-Hukkotai, which means "in My commandments." We must follow all the laws Moshe taught to us. Then God will reward us and protect us, and provide lots of rain, so the crops can grow. God lists things that can happen if the laws aren't followed. God says, "Remember I brought you out of slavery in Egypt and set you free." This is the last parashah in the third book of the Torah, and so we say, "*Hazak, hazak, v'nit-hazek!*—be strong, and be strengthened."

Family Discussion Questions:

1. (Q) We learned about so many laws in the book of Va-Yikra. Which of the laws or commandments do you think is the most important?
2. (Q) What happens to you when you don't follow rules at school? At home?
3. (Q) What do we say when we finish reading one of the books of the Torah? (A) *Hazak, hazak, v'nit-hazek!*

BE-MIDBAR

This is the first parashah is the fourth book of the Torah. This week's parashah is called Be-Midbar. *Be-midbar* means "in the wilderness" or "in the desert." In English this book is called Numbers, because God instructs Moshe to count the number of Jewish people.

God instructs Moshe and Aharon to arrange the twelve tribes of Yisrael (Israel) around the *Mishkan*. The tribe of Levi was to be the group to carry the *Mishkan* and all the things contained inside it. No one else was allowed to put up, take down, or carry the *Mishkan*. At night, each tribe was given a place to set up camp around the *Mishkan* to protect it. And during the day, they walked in the same formation. Moshe thought the people would argue about who would go first, but each tribe had their own special place and their own special jobs. They all worked together to protect the *Mishkan*. The order around the *Mishkan* went like this:

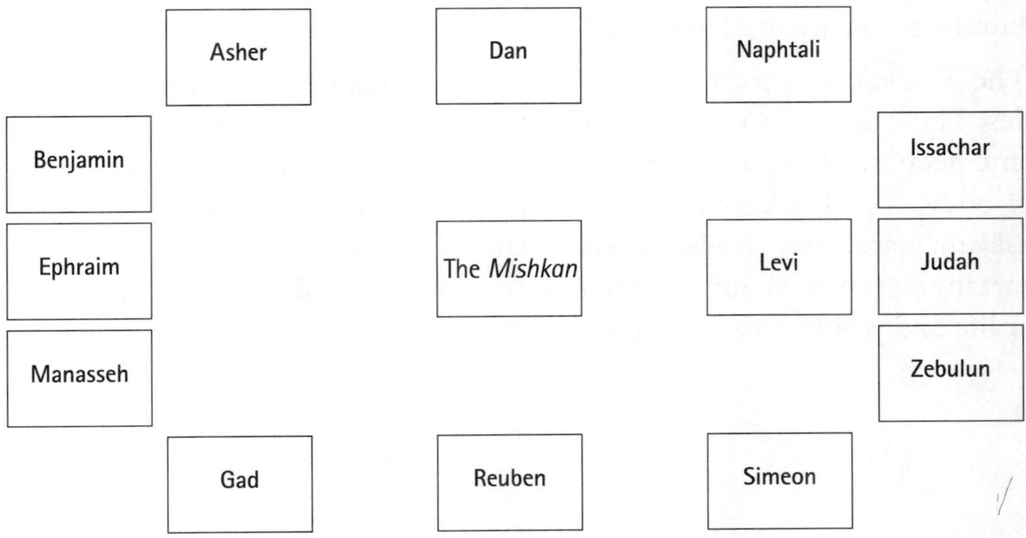

(Bring a banner for each tribe with its symbol [see below] on it when you read this parashah. [See Multimedia Ideas for more suggestions.] Divide the children into twelve groups, each holding a tribe's flag. If you've made a *Mishkan* to use in previous parashiyot, use it now and place it in the center of the twelve groups. As you sing the song below, march in this formation around the *Mishkan*.)

SONG (tune: "Oh My Darling Clementine"—traditional)

We're in the desert, in the desert, in the desert, *be-midbar.*
Be-Midbar we're in the desert, in the desert, *be-midbar.*

We made a pattern around the *Mishkan* with all the twelve tribes,
Made a pattern around the *Mishkan* with all the twelve tribes.

The tribes protected, tribes protected, tribes protected the *Mishkan*.
The tribes protected, tribes protected, tribes protected the *Mishkan*.

Each tribe was also assigned a leader and a special symbol for their flag. Asher's symbol was an olive tree. Benjamin's symbol was a wolf. Dan's was a snake. Gad's was an army camp because Ya'akov blessed him to win all his battles. Manasseh's was an aurochs, which was a large bull with very big horns. Ephraim's was an ox. Simeon's was the gates to the city of Shechem. Zebulun's was a ship. Judah's was a lion. Issachar's was the sun and moon. Naphtali's was a female deer running. Reuben's was a plant with yellow flowers once believed to be magical, called a mandrake. Levi wasn't counted as a tribe, but his symbol was the breastplate (see *Parashat Tetzaveh*) that the *Kohein Gadol* wore. (Later on, when the people were about to enter into the land of Canaan, some of the names of the tribes changed, as a few of the tribes decided to stay behind—see *Parashat Mattot*.)

The *Mishkan* was placed in the center of the tribes. It was protected on all sides. The Ark was in the center of the *Mishkan* and was protected on all sides. Some people say that our heart is like the Torah. Our heart is in the center of our body; it's what keeps us alive. God placed the Torah in the center of the *Mishkan*; placed the *Mishkan* in the center of the twelve tribes, and placed our heart in the center of our body so that the Torah would always be the center of our life and would also help keep us alive.

SONG (tune: "There's a Hole in the Bottom of the Sea"—traditional)

The Torah's in the center of the Ark,
The Torah's in the center of the Ark,
To protect, to protect, to protect the Torah in the Ark.

The Ark is in the center of the *Mishkan,*
The Ark is in the center of the *Mishkan,*
To protect, to protect, the Torah in the Ark in the *Mishkan.*

The *Mishkan*'s in the center of the tribes,
The *Mishkan*'s in the center of the tribes,
To protect, to protect, to protect the *Mishkan.*

MULTIMEDIA IDEAS

"ASK ME" STICKER: Ask me how the tribes protected the *Mishkan.*

CRAFT: The twelve tribes each had a special symbol and flag. Make your own family flag, or make a flag with your Hebrew name on it, and decorate it.

MATH/LANGUAGE: 1) The tribes were broken down by family names. Make a chart of how many people you know with the same name (e.g., using the popular names in your school—Benjamin, Jacob, Joshua, Rachel, Sarah, etc.). Count each category and see which name appears most often.

2) Use patterning shapes to make the twelve tribes' formation around the *Mishkan.*

SCIENCE: 1) *Be-midbar* means "in the wilderness or desert." Learn about the desert. Study desert life, climate, etc.

2) In the sand table, create the formation of the tribes using animals and toys to represent each tribe (of course play in the sand too!)

GAME: There are flashcards available at www.morahmoria.com that could be used as a lotto game if you buy two sets. They are also useful as a visual aid during the acting out of this parashah.

SONG: Sing the "Five Books" song in the Children's Introduction (page 9).

Be-Midbar Family Discussion

(from *Morah, Morah, Teach Me Torah*)

Be-Midbar is the first parashah in the fourth book of the Torah. Be-Midbar means "in the desert or wilderness." In this parashah God instructs Moshe to count the number of people (that's why this book is called Numbers in English).

Moshe is also instructed to arrange the twelve tribes around the *Mishkan* to protect it. The tribes camped out at night and traveled during the day in this formation:

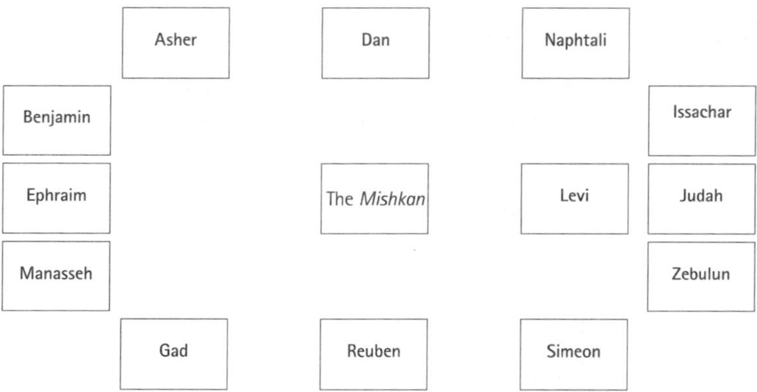

Each tribe was assigned a leader and a symbol for their flags. Asher's was an olive tree, Benjamim's was a wolf, Dan's was a snake, Gad's was an army camp, Manasseh's was an aurochs (big bull with large horns), Ephraim's was an ox, Simeon's was the gates of Shechem, Zebulun's was a ship, Judah's a lion, Naphtali's was a female deer, Reuben's was a mandrake (magical yellow flower), and tribe of Levi was the *Kohein Gadol*'s breastplate. The *Mishkan* and the Levites were in the center of the formation, so the *Mishkan* was protected on all sides.

Family Discussion Questions

1. (Q) Why would each tribe need a leader?
2. (Q) Why was the *Mishkan* in the center?
3. Make a family tree of your own tribe (family).

NASO

Last week we learned about the twelve tribes' formation around the *Mishkan* to protect it. This week we read Parashat Naso, which means "taking a count of the people."

We know that the Jewish people were traveling in the desert. God showed that God was with the Jewish people in the form of a cloud by day and fire by night (just like God did as they left Egypt). If God wanted the people to move, then the fire/cloud would move, and then the people would know where to go. (The Children of Israel had their own GPS system!) Each tribe was assigned a job and a place to be around the *Mishkan*.

The Levites were told that they were the tribe in charge of moving the *Mishkan*. God taught the Levites exactly how to take care of the Mishkan, how to take it down for traveling, how to put it together. and how to move the Ark. Each tribe was instructed to bring gifts to the *Mishkan* for God for twelve days. They were to bring one gold pan, one silver bowl, one silver basin, one bull, two oxen, five goats, five lambs, and five rams.

SONG (tune: "The Bear went Over the Mountain"—traditional)

One silver dish, and one golden pan,
one bull, two oxen, and five lambs.
one silver basin, five goats, and five rams.
Were the gifts brought to the *Mishkan*.

The tribes all brought many gifts.
They brought the gifts for twelve days.
These were the gifts for the *Mishkan*,
As instructed by God.

God then reminds our people to be kind. If they are not kind to someone, then they must say they're sorry and pay for the damages they caused (even if it was an accident).

The *Kohanim* were taught the *Birkat Kohanim*, the priestly blessing. This special blessing the *Kohanim* gave to the people is still done today on Rosh Hashanah, Sukkot, Pesah, and Shavuot in some synagogues. It's called dukhenen—remember we learned about that in parashat Tetzaveh and Va-Yikra? The *Kohanim* hold their hands in a special way, and say:

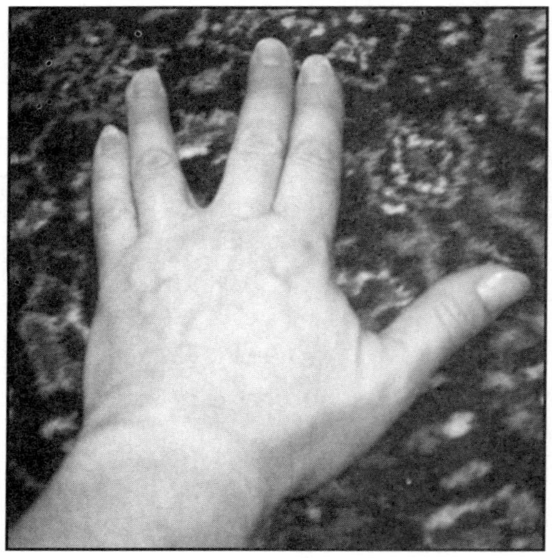

"May God bless you and protect you.

May God deal kindly with you.

May God shine God's face upon you
and bring you peace."

This is same blessing parents say to their children on Friday night.

At the end of Naso, we learn that Moshe hears God's voice through the center of the Ark (*Aron ha-Kodesh*), between the cherubim (angels).

MULTIMEDIA IDEAS

"ASK ME" STICKER: Ask me how the Jewish people knew where to go in the desert.

MATH: 1) God instructs the twelve tribes to bring gifts to the *Mishkan*. Collect those things from your housekeeping corner and play animals. Count: How many in all? How many of each thing?

2) There were twelve tribes and they gave gifts for twelve days. Count to twelve in English and Hebrew. Can you make a group of twelve things?

FINE MOTOR: Try holding your hands like the *Kohanim*. It's hard to do!

LANGUAGE: Talk about the blessing the *Kohanim* said to the people. Parents still say it to their children on Shabbat. Practice learning the blessings (English or Hebrew). It's found at the end of the *Amidah* (*Sh'moneh Esreh*).

CRAFT: 1) Make a hamsa. The hamsa is sometimes called the *hamesh* hand, or the *yad* of God. It was used to protect people from the Evil Eye. It is an inverted hand with the thumb and pinkie sticking out a little bit; usually it has an eye in the center.

2) Trace your hand in the shape that the *Kohanim* put their hands when blessing the people.

Parashat Naso Family Discussion

(from *Morah, Morah, Teach Me Torah*)

We know that the Jewish people were traveling through the desert. Naso means "taking a counting of" all the people. God helped show them the way by having a cloud to follow by day and a pillar of fire to lead the way by night. When the cloud/fire moved, that was how the people knew when to move and where to move. The Levites were told that they were the tribe in charge of moving the *Mishkan* and were taught exactly how to move it. Where the Torah was kept was called the Holy of Holies. Each tribe was told to bring gifts to the *Mishkan* for twelve days. They were to bring a one silver bowl, one golden pan, a bull, two oxen, five lambs, one silver basin, five goats and five rams. The *Kohanim* said the priestly blessing just as they do today, which says that "God will bless you and protect you. God will shine God's face upon you and bring you peace."

Family Discussion Questions:

1. (Q) How did the people know where and when to move across the desert? (A) A cloud moved by day and fire by night.
2. (Q) How did the people show their devotion to the *Mishkan*? (A) By bringing gifts.
3. (Q) Whose job was it to say the priestly blessing that is still recited today? (A) The *Kohanim*.
4. (Q) Have you ever been blessed by your parents on Shabbat? How did you feel afterwards?

BE-HA'ALOTEKHA

Last week we learned about the *Kohanim* blessing, and the gifts brought to the *Mishkan*.

This week's parashah is called Be-Ha'alotekha, which means "raise the light"; it reminds us of the lights on the seven-branched menorah. The Children of Israel were almost ready to move on. They had been camped in the desert at *Har Sinai* for such a long time, and they wanted to get to a place they could call home. As they traveled, they followed the cloud that remained over the *Mishkan* during the day and the pillar of fire that appeared at night. When the cloud stayed over the *Mishkan* for a long time, the people stayed in one place for a long time. When the cloud moved, the people moved.

The *Kohanim*, who were like their teachers, prepared them for their journey. First, Moshe reminded the people of the menorah and lit the menorah. The people were reminded about the laws of Pesah (Passover).

Next, God said to Moshe, "Moshe, make two trumpets out of silver to call the people. Teach them what the different sounds of the trumpets mean. If the *Kohanim* want the people to gather around together, they will blow a long blast of one trumpet. Two trumpets blasting together quickly will mean it is time to move on. Many short blasts on the trumpet will mean that the people have to go to war with their enemies. The trumpets will also be blown on joyous holidays."

MOVEMENT ACTIVITY: Using a pretend horn, play a game moving around the room and listening to the blasts of the horn. A short blast means they can move (skip, hop, run, walk, jump, etc.) around the room. A long blast means they should come together in a group in front of the teacher. Two short blasts means to run in a circle. You could also use this when lining up at the door or for cleanup. Children can take turns being the *Kohein Gadol*. (Hap Palmer has a song called "Teacher Who Could Not Talk" that is a similar concept: www.happalmer.com.)

SONG (tune: "I've Been Working on the Railroad"—traditional)

I've been teaching all the laws, to the Jews
I've been teaching all the laws, so they'll know what to do
God asked for a silver trumpet
To gather the people around
Different blasts mean different things
Listen for the sound:

Chorus: Have the *Kohein* blow, have the *Kohein* blow,
have the *Kohein* blow the trumpet
Have the *Kohein* blow, have the *Kohein* blow,
have the *Kohein* blow the horn.

One long blast means come together,
Two blasts quickly move on,
Many short blasts means it's time for war,
Listen to the horn.

(Repeat chorus)

Everyone lined up to start walking. However, just as they were ready to go, the people started complaining again. They complained about the food they were eating. They remembered the delicious foods they ate in Egypt. But in the desert they ate only manna, which God sent down for them to eat so they wouldn't starve. But now they wanted meat to eat, and fish and vegetables and fruit. They all started shouting and complaining at once.

(Optional: Have the children all complain about something all at once.)

Moshe was quite angry, and he looked to God to see what to do. "What am I supposed to do? How can I give them meat?" asked Moshe.

All of a sudden, a big wind blew, and when the people looked up, they saw quail flying everywhere. Quail are a kind of bird. God sent so many quail that the people ate and ate and ate until they got so sick.

Next, God said to Moshe, "Moshe, gather seven of your wisest men. I will make them even wiser, and they will help you lead the people."

Moshe's brother Aharon and his sister Miriam became jealous that God spoke only to Moshe. "Why does God speak only to Moshe and not to us?"

And they started saying mean things (*lashon ha-ra*) about Moshe and his wife, Tzipporah. God became angry with Miriam and came down in a pillar of cloud to speak to Moshe, Aharon, and Miriam. God said, "Only **I** choose who I wish to speak to, and **I** choose who will be a prophet."

And when the cloud lifted, Miriam was punished and left with *tzara'at* (spots). (Remember, we learned about it in parashat Tazria?) God caused Miriam to have a skin disease. Her arms turned all white, and she was sick. Aharon begged forgiveness from Moshe, and Moshe asked God to forgive Miriam and to help her heal. And, of course, in seven days, Miriam was better and NOW the people of Israel could start their journey.

MULTIMEDIA IDEAS

"ASK ME" STICKER: Ask me how the people knew where to go in the desert.

CRAFT: Design a horn using cardboard, poster board, or paper, and insert a party blower horn at the end.

DRAMATIC PLAY: Use or make bird puppets to act out the story when God sends down the quail to eat.

LANGUAGE: Aharon and Miriam were jealous of Moshe that he received all the attention from God and from the Jewish people. Talk about a time that you were jealous, and write down the ideas.

MATH: Pretend to march around the room in an order, just as the tribes walked in an order in the desert. Order the children from smallest to tallest, or place them in "families" or groups, such as all the children with straight hair in the first group, all with curly hair in another group, all the children with light-colored hair behind that group, etc.

STORY: *Say It with Zest* by Mindy Shapiro (saying kind words).

Parashat Be-Ha'alotekha Family Discussion

(from *Morah, Morah, Teach Me Torah*)

Be-ha'alotekha means "to raise the light." In this parashah the people were ready to move on through the desert, following the cloud by day and fire by night. The *Kohanim* prepared them for their long journey. They reminded the people of the menorah and lit the menorah. They were also reminded of the laws of Pesah. God told Moshe to make two trumpets out of silver with which to call the people. We learn that different blasts of the trumpet meant different things. One long blast meant for the people to gather around together near the *Kohanim*. Two trumpets blasting together meant it was time to move on. And many short blasts meant that the people had to go to war with their enemies. The trumpets were also blown on joyous holidays. As the people were traveling, they began to complain about being hungry and not having good food, like they had in Egypt. God was angry and sent a big wind, and quail began to fly everywhere for the people to eat. The people ate until they got sick. Moshe's brother Aharon and his sister Miriam became jealous that God spoke only to Moshe, and they began to say unkind things about Moshe. Miriam was punished by getting a skin disease until Moshe asked forgiveness from God to heal Miriam. Now the people could move on.

Family Discussion Questions:

1. (Q) How did the *Kohanim* tell the people what they needed to do? (A) By blowing the trumpet.
2. (Q) What holiday do we blow a trumpet of sorts? (A) Rosh ha-Shanah and the end of Yom Kippur.
3. (Q) What happened when the people complained about not having enough good food to eat? (A) God sent quails and the people ate them until they got sick.
4. (Q) Have you ever been jealous of someone?

SHELAH LEKHA

In last week's parashah we learned about being jealous and how ungrateful *B'nai Yisrael* had become. Do you remember the tenth commandment (Do not covet), "Be happy with what you have"?

This week we read Parashat Shelah Lekha. The word *shelah* means "to send;" *Shelah Lekha* means "send you." And that's just what happened. God sent the people to the Land of Israel. In those days, it wasn't called Israel. It was called Canaan. But what did they know about Canaan? Nothing! So Moshe sent out twelve spies to go into Canaan and look over the land to find out what kinds of foods grew there and what the people were like who lived there. Were they friendly? Did the cities have high walls surrounding them?

Why do you think he sent "twelve" spies? Do you remember earlier what twelve represented? The twelve tribes, and the leaders of each tribe were the twelve spies who went into Canaan.

They stayed in Canaan for forty days, and when they came back, they were carrying fruits: pomegranates, grapes, and figs (some of the seven species that grow in Israel). They reported that the land was flowing with "milk and honey."

SONG 1 (tune: "London Bridges"—traditional)

Twelve spies went to Canaan, to Canaan, to Canaan
twelve spies went to Canaan, what would they see?

They stayed in Canaan for forty days, forty days, forty days
They stayed in Canaan for forty days, this is what they found.

Pomegranates, figs and grapes, figs and grapes, figs and grapes
Pomegranates, figs and grapes, a land of milk and honey.

SONG 2: Israeli traditional by Eliyahu Gamliel

Eretz zavat h̲alav—oohh ahh—h̲alav u'd'vash.
(This is the land flowing with milk and honey.)

(Add the dance that goes along with this song. Shlock Rock has a fun version of this song on the CD *Shlock Rock For Kids Party Time!*)

Ten of the spies also talked about the people living there. They were very scared. Some of the spies said to Moshe, "The people in Canaan are giants, and they are very strong and powerful. We are like grasshoppers to them."

B'nai Yisrael became very afraid and cried out, "No, we cannot go into this land! We would have been better off in Egypt. Let us go back to Egypt!"

God heard this and was very angry at the people. "Why do they not trust Me? I have taken them out of slavery. I have provided them with food. I have led them to a land they can call their own. No matter what I do, it's not good enough," God said to Moshe.

With that, God punished the people. He would not allow them to go into the land of Canaan for forty years. During that time, they would have to wander in the desert.

SONG (tune: "She'll Be Coming 'Round the Mountain"—traditional)

There are giants in the land of Canaan, Oy Vey!
There are giants in the land of Canaan
The spies all are frightened
The people are scared also
"Let's all go back to Egypt instead."
Now God becomes angry with the Jews, Oy Vey!
Now God becomes angry with the Jews
So for forty years they'll wander
They'll wander in the desert
Then they'll settle in the land of Canaan.

Does God forgive the Jewish people? Of course! But before they enter the land, God must teach them some new rules about how to live in this new land.

For one thing, when the people settle in, they must bake bread. What kind of bread do you think they make? They bake h̲allah, and when the bread is ready to be baked, a small portion of the dough must be torn off and set aside for God. This is a mitzvah, and even today, many people still separate a piece of the dough and burn it in the oven after making a special *brakhah* (blessing) (see Multimedia Ideas).

Another thing that Moshe told the people to do was to make *tzitzit* on the corners of a special garment. The *tzitzit* are fringes that were attached to the four corners of a garment. Today we wear a *tallit* with the *tzitzit* attached to it when we pray, and some men wear the *tzitzit* under their clothes every day, and not just when they pray. God commanded, "You shall wear the *tzitzit* and then you will remember who you are, and you will remember the commandments I gave you to make you holy. Remember, I am the Eternal who took you out of Egypt. I am God."

MULTIMEDIA IDEAS

"ASK ME" STICKER: Ask me what land is "flowing with milk and honey" (*halav u'd'vash*).

GEOGRAPHY: Laminate a picture of what Israel looked like when it was Canaan. A picture of this map can be found in the back of the *Etz Hayyim humash* (or at www.originofnations.org, click on Migration of Israel). Show a map of Israel today and compare the two.

GAME: Play a game of "I Spy." Choose a couple of "leaders/spies" and send them out of the room. Hide play fruit around the room. Have the spies come into the room and find the fruit of the land.

SNACK TIME: Try eating pomegranate, figs, and grapes. Learn the different *brakhot* (blessings) for eating fruit.

Here is the *brakhah* we say when eating fruits and vegetables that grow in the ground.

בָּרוּךְ אַתָּה יי אֱלֹהֵינוּ מֶלֶךְ הָעוֹלָם בּוֹרֵא פְּרִי הָאֲדָמָה.

Barukh Attah Adonai Eloheinu Melekh ha-Olam Borei pri ha-adamah.

Praised are You, Eternal, our God Ruler of the Cosmos, Who creates the fruit of the ground.

Here is the *brakhah* we say when eating fruits that grow on a tree.

בָּרוּךְ אַתָּה יי אֱלֹהֵינוּ מֶלֶךְ הָעוֹלָם בּוֹרֵא פְּרִי הָעֵץ.

Barukh Attah Adonai, Eloheinu Melekh ha-Olam Borei pri ha-etz.

Praised are You, Eternal, our God Ruler of the Cosmos, Who creates the fruit of the tree.

MATH/SCIENCE/COOKING: Bake hallah (see Bereshit for a recipe), making sure you separate an olive-sized portion of the dough and say the *brakhah*:

בָּרוּךְ אַתָּה יי אֱלֹהֵינוּ מֶלֶךְ הָעוֹלָם אֲשֶׁר קִדְּשָׁנוּ בְּמִצְוֹתָיו
וְצִוָּנוּ לְהַפְרִישׁ חַלָּה.

Barukh Attah Adonai, Eloheinu Melekh ha-Olam asher kidshanu b'mitzvotav v'tzivanu l'hafrish hallah.

Blessed are You, Eternal, our God, Ruler of the universe, Who has sanctified us with commandments and commanded us to separate hallah.

CRAFT: 1) Make a tallit; add yarn to the corners. Practice tying knots on the fringes.

2) Make a hallah out of play dough: Have the children make the play dough, and then braid it. Save one to use in your family corner (after baking it).

You can also make two hallot out of six recycled knee-high nylon stockings. Stuff them with poly-fill (available at craft or sewing stores). Take three and braid them together. Sew or glue the ends together. Then repeat with the other three. Design a hallah cover from an old T-shirt to use in your housekeeping corner. By using recycled materials, you are doing the mitzvah of *bal tash'hit*.

Parashat Shelah Lekha Family Discussion

(from *Morah, Morah, Teach Me Torah*)

Shelah Lekha means "send you." The people were on their way to the Land of Israel, but in those days it was called Canaan. But what did the people know about this land? Nothing. So Moshe sent twelve spies into Canaan to look over the land, to see what kinds of fruits and vegetables could grow there, and to see if the people were friendly. They stayed in Canaan for forty days, and when they came back they were carrying pomegranates, grapes and figs. They reported that the land was "flowing with milk and honey." They also reported that the people living there were giants and were very strong and powerful. The people were afraid and wanted to turn back and return to Egypt. This made God angry, and as a result, God wouldn't let them go into Canaan for forty years. Of course, God forgave the Jewish people, but they would need to know more rules about how to live in this new land. They would have to learn to bake bread, and a small portion of the bread they baked should be torn off and set aside as a gift to God. Moshe was instructed to have the people make *tzitzit* to wear on the corners of their garments, so that they would remember that they are *B'nai Yisrael* and remember the commandments and keep them holy.

Family Discussion Questions:

1. (Q) How did the people learn about the land of Canaan? And what did they learn? (A) Twelve spies were sent into the land. They found pomegranates, grapes, and figs and reported that the people there were like giants but the land flowed with milk and honey—*eretz zavat halav u'd'vash*.
2. (Q) Were the people happy to go into this land? What happened to them? (A) No, they were scared. They were punished by not being allowed to go into Canaan for forty years.
3. (Q) Have you ever been afraid about going to a new place? How did you overcome your fear?

KORAH

Last week we learned that the Israelites wandered for forty years in the wilderness, or desert, as punishment for not trusting that Canaan was safe to enter. They were also instructed to wear *tzitzit*.

This week we read Parashat Korah. Korah is named after a member of the Levi tribe. Korah thought it wasn't fair that Moshe and Aharon had all the most important jobs as the leaders. He wanted to be the leader! But think back, did Moshe and Aharon choose to be the leaders? No! God chose them! Korah gathered a group of people who supported him, and together they went to see Moshe and Aharon.

"I want to be the leader of the *Mishkan*. Why should Aharon get to do everything?" asked Korah.

Moshe answered, "God will choose."

God did choose. God made the ground open up and swallow Korah and his followers!

SONG (tune: "Oh Do you Know the Muffin Man"—traditional)

Korah wanted to be boss, to be boss, to be boss
Korah wanted to be boss, instead of Moshe and Aharon.

God opened up the ground, up the ground, up the ground
God opened up the ground and swallowed up Korah.

God chose Aharon, Aharon, Aharon
God chose Aharon as leader of the *Mishkan*.

Aharon then went to the altar to make a gift offering to say that the community was sorry for questioning God. Moshe said to the tribes, "Every leader of every tribe must take their staffs and write the name of the tribe on it, and put them in the Holy Ark [*Aron ha-Kodesh*]. God will choose who will lead the Israelites."

Then everyone said the Shema and went to bed.

(Let's all sing the Shema together: *Shema Yisrael Adonai Eloheinu, Adonai Ehad.*)

The next morning Moshe went into the Holy of Holies and gathered the staffs. Aharon's staff had begun to grow overnight into a beautiful almond tree. It had branches, leaves, flowers, and almonds growing on it. So Aharon was again chosen by God and continued to lead the Jewish people.

God gave the *Kohanim* more jobs to perform. However, because the Levi tribe questioned God, they would not receive any land when the people entered Canaan. All the farmers would have to share all that they had with the Levites.

SONG (tune: "B-I-N-G-O"—traditional)

God gave us lots of special gifts that we must share with others
S-H-A-R-E (3x)
We share all that we have.

(variation:
God gave us many gifts to share with the Levites
S-H-A-R-E (3x)
We share all that we have.)

MULTIMEDIA IDEAS

"ASK ME" STICKER: Ask me who God chose as the leader (or boss) of the Jewish people.

CRAFT: God made Aharon's staff turn into an almond tree. Make an almond tree—take a tree branch from outside and glue on green tissue-paper leaves and pink-tissue or silk flower petals for the blossoms. If there are no allergies, hot-glue some real almonds in their shells onto the branch. Mount it into a glob of clay and use as a centerpiece for Shabbat.

GAME: Play "Follow the Leader." (Korah was not a good follower. Let's see how well WE can do!)

SCIENCE: Overnight, freeze a block of ice tinted a dark color, (like the ground) or use cola, (it expands, so don't fill the container too full). To show how the ground opened up and swallowed up Korah, pour hot water (almost boiling) over one spot on the ice to create a hole. Talk about freezing and melting. Try different ways to experiment with the ice. Predict what will happen and chart the results. (Try kosher salt, sugar, cold water, etc.)

Parashat Korah Family Discussions

Korah was the name of one of the members of the Levi tribe whom this parashah is about. Korah thought it wasn't fair that Moshe and Aharon had all the important jobs as leaders. Korah wanted to be a leader, too. But remember, Moshe and Aharon did not choose to be the leaders—God chose them. Then the earth opened up and swallowed Korah and his followers. Aharon goes to the altar to make a gift offering to apologize for the community's questioning God. Moshe tells each tribe leader to write their names on their staffs and put them in the Holy of Holies. God will choose a leader for the Israelites. Overnight, Aharon's staff had begun to grow into a beautiful almond tree with leaves, flowers, and even almonds! Again, Aharon was chosen. God gives the *Kohanim* more jobs to do. However, because the tribe of Levi questioned God, they will not receive any land when the Jewish people finally enter the land of Canaan. The community must share what they have with the Levites.

Family Discussion Questions:

1. (Q) Why was Korah unhappy? (A) Korah thought it was unfair that only Moshe and Aharon got to be the leaders.
2. (Q) How did Moshe and Aharon get to be leaders? (A) God chose them.
3. (Q) What happened when all the tribe leaders placed their staffs into the Holy of Holies? (A) Aharon's grew into an almond tree.
4. (Q) How did God punish the Levi tribe for questioning God? (A) They would be given no land of their own to farm when they got to Canaan.
5. (Q) Do you ever wish you could be the boss of your family?

H̲UKKAT

In last week's parashah, the ground swallowed up Korah̲ and his followers because they questioned God. Oy, will *B'nai Yisrael* (the Jewish people) ever learn?

In Parashat H̲ukkat, which means "the laws of," God instructs Moshe to have the *Kohanim* give an all red, young cow (a heifer) as a gift offering. The *Kohein Gadol* must first take a bath and wash his clothes before he makes the offering.

SONG (tune: "This is the Way We Wash Our Clothes"—traditional)

This is the way the *Kohein* bathed, *Kohein* bathed, *Kohein* bathed
This is the way the *Kohein* bathed
To give God the gift offering.

Once on the right and once on the left,
Once on the right and once on the left,
Once on the right and once on the left
"*Al n'tilat yadayim*".

This is the way they washed their clothes, washed their clothes,
washed their clothes
This is the way they washed their clothes
To give God the gift offering.

Some rabbis say the gift offering of the all-red cow was to say "I'm sorry" for the sins of the golden calf (see Parashat Ki Tissa). The red cow had to be perfect, with no boo-boos and no scars, and every hair on its body had to be red! That must have been hard to find.

God also instructs Moshe what to do when someone dies. The body must be treated with respect and washed; special prayers are to be said, and then the people who took care of the dead person had to wash themselves and their clothing very well. After God explained these rules to Moshe, Miriam died. It was a very sad time for Moshe and Aharon because Miriam was their sister.

It's been said that because Miriam was so important, a miraculous well of water followed the Jewish people through the desert to give them water. When Miriam died, the well dried up, and there was no water.

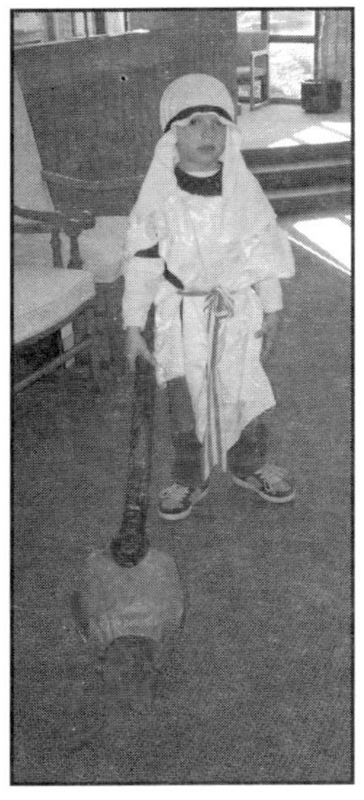

Since there was no more water, the Jewish people started to complain AGAIN about being thirsty.

"We were better off in Egypt [*Mitzrayim*]. Why did you bring us so far to die?" kvetched the people.

Moshe then complains to God. God says to Moshe, "Speak to the rock, and water [the waters of Meribah] will flow out of the rock." But Moses is so angry and tired of listening to the people complain that he hit the rock two times, and water came splashing out. The Israelites now have plenty of water, but God is really angry! "I told you to speak to the rock, not hit it! You and Aharon will be punished for not doing what I asked you to do! You will NOT be allowed to enter the promised land of Canaan [Israel]!"

SONG (tune: "Eency Weency Spider"—traditional)

All the Jewish people kvetched and moaned
"We are thirsty, we were better off back home!"
"Speak to a rock, that's what you have to do"
But Moshe hit the rock two times
"So, no Canaan for you!"

God then tells Moshe that it is time for Aharon to die also. Moshe is told, "Take Aharon's son Eleazar and go up on the mountain. Tell Aharon to wear the special *Kohein Gadol* clothing." When they reach the place that God shows them, Aharon dies.

This is a very sad parashah; first Miriam dies, then Aharon. They lived a long life and were very good people. *B'nai Yisrael* are very sad. They cried for Aharon, their leader, and said, "He was a very holy man [a *tzaddik*]. He helped us to be good and helped us make friends with our enemies. We will miss him!" God now makes Eleazer (Aharon's son) the new *Kohein Gadol*.

After a while, the people began to complain AGAIN. This time they were tired of eating manna and quail. God sent snakes to bite the people who kept kvetching (complaining). So, again, the people said "I'm sorry." As a reminder, God told Moshe to make a staff (a stick) out of copper shaped like a snake. Whenever someone felt like complaining, they just had to look at the staff and remember all the snakes, and they would be happy with what they had. (That's the tenth commandment!)

MULTIMEDIA IDEAS

"ASK ME" STICKER: Ask me what happened when Moshe hit the rock.

CRAFT: 1) Make a papier-mâché rock out of an inflated balloon covered with newspaper dipped in a paste. Papier-mâché goo can be made by either using flour and water (1:3 ratio) mixed into a paste or using liquid starch. After the "rock" hardens overnight, fill it with blue crepe-paper streamers and blue confetti (and, of course, candy if you want to). Then paint it gray and allow it to dry again. (It's like a piñata.) When you act out the parashah, hit the rock and watch the "water" splash out.

2) Some people like to include a Miriam's cup at their Seder table to symbolize the miracle of Miriam's well of water in the desert. The Babylonian Talmud (Sotah 9b) says, "If it wasn't for the righteousness of the women of that generation, we would not have been redeemed from Egypt." Make a Miriam's cup and talk about all the different women with a well involved in their lives, such as Rivka, Rachel, and Miriam. One idea to make a Miriam's cup is to use a plastic wine glass from the party store. Paint glue or Modge Podge on the cup, and cover with tissue paper pieces to make a stained glass effect. Paint over the tissue paper again with glue or Modge Podge to give the cup a "glazed" affect.

MOVEMENT: Try to slither like snakes! Divide the group in half and make one group the snakes and the other group the people. Play freeze tag, with the snakes trying to catch the people. If a snake touches you, FREEZE!

HOUSEKEEPING: Take out your dolls and doll clothes, and wash them like the *Kohein Gadol* before he gave a gift offering.

GAME: Since Moshe made a mistake (a "whoops"), play the hand game: "Moshe, Moshe, Moshe, Moshe, whoops, Moshe, whoops, Moshe, Moshe, Moshe, Moshe." Starting with your pinkie finger, tap each finger and swoop down to your thumb on the "whoops" part.

Parashat Hukkat Family Discussion

(from *Morah, Morah, Teach Me Torah*)

In this parashah God instructs Moshe to have the *Kohanim* give an all-red calf (heifer) as a gift offering. The *Kohein Gadol* must first take a bath and wash his clothes before making the offering. This offering of the calf was to say "I'm sorry" for the sins of the golden calf. The red cow had to be perfect (no boo-boos). The people are also taught what to do when a person dies; the body should be treated with respect and washed, and special prayers should be said. In this parashah, Miriam dies. The well of water that flourished while Miriam was alive dried up, and there was a lack of water. Again the people complained about being thirsty and having no water. God speaks to Moshe and tells him to speak to a rock and the waters of Meribah will flow out of the rock. But Moshe is angry and tired of listening to the people complain, so he hits the rock two times. Water begins to flow from the rock, but God is angry with Moshe for not obeying the directions and not doing what he was told. "You will NOT be allowed to enter the land of Canaan," Moshe was told. Aharon also dies in this parashah, and his son Eleazar becomes the new *Kohein Gadol*. The people are complaining again, because they are tired of eating manna and quail. This time God sends snakes to bite the people who are complaining. They should "be happy with what they have!" (remember the tenth commandment).

Family Discussion Questions:

1. (Q) Have you ever seen a cow that is all red?
2. (Q) Why was God angry with Moshe? (A) He didn't follow God's directions and speak to the rock.
3. (Q) What happens when you complain about things a lot? Do you remember what the tenth commandment is?

BALAK

In last week's parashah, we learned all about what the *Kohanim* had to do before making a gift offering. Both Miriam and Aharon died. It was a sad parashah.

In Parashat Balak, which was the name of a king, we read how the people of Israel had to travel through different cities in order to get to Canaan. Sometimes the leaders of those cities wouldn't let them pass through. The Jewish people were strangers to them, and they were afraid of the people because there were so many of them. Then the people of Israel came to one of the strongest countries, Moav. The king of Moav was named Balak. (Use puppets to act it out, or have the children play the parts.) Balak said, "I'm afraid that you, the people of Israel will come into my country and attack us." What do you think he should do?

He gathered up his wisest men, and he hired a fortune-teller named Balaam. "Balaam, your job is to stop the Israelites from entering Moav by making curses over them. If you tell them something bad will happen to them, then they might become afraid and believe it will really happen."

Remember, God promised the Jewish people to always take care of them and to protect them? God spoke to Balaam and told him, "Go with Balak to speak to the Israelites, but you will say only what I want you to say."

Whom should Balaam listen to, God or Balak? In the morning Balaam saddled up his donkey and rode to the top of the mountain to speak his curses. God saw this and made the donkey go down the wrong path over and over again. God made an angel appear, to stand in front of the donkey and to make the donkey turn down a different path. Only the donkey could see the angel. This, of course, made Balaam angry, and he yelled at the donkey and hit the donkey.

(Everyone, yell at the donkey: "What's the matter with you?")

To his surprise, the donkey began to speak: "What did I ever do to you to make you hit me?" Balaam apologized to the donkey, "I'm sorry for hitting you, donkey." And he went to the top of the mountain and begin speaking to the Israelites who are at the bottom. But every time Balaam started to curse the Israelites, God did a miracle and changed Balaam's tongue so that something kind comes out of his mouth. Each time, he blessed the people instead of cursing them. He said, "How lovely are your tents, Ya'akov and your house of worship [your Mishkan], Yisrael."

מַה טֹּבוּ אֹהָלֶיךָ יַעֲקֹב מִשְׁכְּנֹתֶיךָ יִשְׂרָאֵל.

Mah tovu ohalekha Ya'akov, Mishk'notekha Yisrael.

MULTIMEDIA IDEAS

"ASK ME" STICKER: Ask me what miracle God did to Balaam.

SONG: Teach the prayer *Mah Tovu*. When you teach *Mah Tovu*, hold up a large tallit and let the children stand under it, like a big tent.

Mah tovu ohalekha Ya'akov, Mishk'notekha Yisrael.

It means "How lovely are your tents, Ya'akov [Jacob] and your *Mishkan, Yisrael* [Israel]." *Mah Tovu* is said daily during *Shaharit* (morning prayers). When we come into a synagogue on Shabbat morning, this is often one of the first prayers we recite. It's a prayer that tells how **good** it is to be in the house of God (**Tov** is the Hebrew word for "good").

LANGUAGE: (1) Have the children listen carefully to the words in the prayer *Mah Tovu* and pick out the words they recognize. Emphasize the words they might know, such as *Yisrael*, or *Ya'akov* or *Tov*. (Hold your hands like a tent when you say the prayer.)

2) It is a mitzvah, *tza'ar ba'alei hayyim*, to be kind to animals. Balaam hit the donkey. Is that kind? Talk about ways people are mean to animals. Then write down all the ways to be kind to animals.

CRAFT: Make tents and decorate them: Decorate a large half circle, with paint (cotton swabs work well to paint with). Cut one slit halfway across the circle and roll into a cone (or teepee shape) and staple closed. (How beautiful is your tent!)

MOVEMENT/DRAMATIC PLAY: Take a hike to the top of a hill and act out the story.

Parashat Balak Family Discussion

(from *Morah, Morah, Teach Me Torah*)

Balak is the name of the king of Moav. The Children of Israel had to travel through many cities to get to Canaan. Sometimes the leaders of those cities wouldn't let them come through, since they were strangers to their land and they were afraid of them. When the Jewish people were going to enter Moav, the king, Balak, was afraid that they would attack them. So he gathered up his wisest men and he hired a fortune-teller named Balaam to go to the Israelites and tell them something bad would happen if they came into Moav, so maybe they would be afraid and not enter. But remember, God promised to protect the Jewish people! God spoke to Balaam and told him to go with Balak to speak to the Israelites and say only what God told him to say. Who should Balaam listen to, God or Balak? In the morning, Balaam saddled up his donkey and rode to the top of the mountain. God saw this and made the donkey go down the wrong path and made an angel appear in front of the donkey (that only the donkey could see). Balaam was angry and yelled at the donkey and hit him. To his surprise the donkey spoke to Balaam, asking what he did to make him hit him. After he apologized to the donkey, he tried to speak curses to the Israelites, but God changed his tongue so that only nice words came from his mouth. He said, "*Mah tovu ohalekha Ya'akov, Mishk'notekha Yisrael.* How lovely are your tents, Ya'akov, and your house of worship, Israel."

Family Discussion Questions:

1. (Q) Who was Balak? (A) The king of Moav.
2. (Q) What did God do when Balaam wanted to say unkind things to the Jewish people? (A) God caused Balaam to bless the Israelites instead of cursing them.
3. Sing some prayers together like the Shema or *Mah Tovu*. Listen for words you know.

PINHAS

In last week's parashah we learned how Balaam blessed *B'nai Yisrael* instead of cursing them, and said *Mah Tovu*. (Let's sing *Mah Tovu* again before we read the next parashah.)

This parashah is about Pinhas, the son of Eleazar, who is one of Aharon's sons and one of the *Kohanim*. In this parashah Pinhas receives a very special honor. He becomes one of the leaders and helps Moshe to guide the Israelites into Canaan. It's time to count the number of people again to see how many are left to enter the "Promised Land." Moshe says to the people, "When you get into Canaan, the land will be divided among the families. Every man will have a portion of land."

Remember, in the story of Ya'akov (Jacob) and Esav (Esau), their father's land would be given to the oldest son. In those days, the land was given to the men of the family. The mommies of the families cooked and took care of the house and children. They didn't own land. How many people have mommies who work outside of the house today? Today, mommies can do anything; they go to college, they have jobs and they can own land.

In this parashah, there were five daughters of a man named Zelophehad. (Choose five girls to be the five daughters and one boy to be Moshe.) The daughters come to Moshe and say, "We have no father and we have no brothers to receive land. But we believe that we should also be given a piece of land." God agreed, and land was given to the five daughters of Zelophehad.

SONG (tune: "Farmer in the Dell"—traditional; lyrics by Diane Holsten)

Zelophehad was a man, Zelophehad was a man
Zelophehad had five daughters, and they wanted some land.

The men got all the land, the men got all the land
But the daughters had no father then, and they wanted some land.

They asked Moshe for help, they asked Moshe for help
He thought it through, "I understand." He gave the daughters some land.

Then God said to Moshe, "Climb to the top of the mountain so you can see the land of Canaan. Remember, you will not be able to enter into Canaan because you are being punished for not following my directions of speaking to the rock to get water."

Remember, in Parashat Hukkat, that Moshe hit the rock two times to get water, which made God angry.

"Who will lead the Jewish people if I am not allowed to go to Canaan?" Moshe asks.

Yehoshua (Joshua), who was Moshe's helper, was appointed the next leader of the Jewish people.

Before they are allowed to enter the land, the people are once again reminded to celebrate Shabbat, Rosh ha-Shanah, Yom Kippur, Sukkot, Pesah, and Shavuot.

MULTIMEDIA IDEAS

"ASK ME" STICKER: Ask me who will be the new leader for the Jewish people.

MATH: Since the counting of the people was so important in this parashah, do some counting activities:

1) Have dice available for the children to roll and count the number of dots on the dice. Prepare matching number cards to choose the appropriate card that matches the number of dots on the dice.

2) Play with dominos, or play a board game where you have to count the appropriate number of spaces to move.

MOVEMENT: On a square box, write a number (or put a different number of dots) on each of the sides of the box (like a large die). Children stand in a circle and take turns tossing the numbered cube. The child who tossed the cube counts the number of dots, or reads the numeral that is face up and then chooses some kind of movement to do that the rest of the children will then copy that number of times.

LANGUAGE: Because the women (the five daughters) were considered important members of the family of Israel and were given land, it is a good time to recall the other important women in the Torah.

Prepare a "trivia" type game or a game of charades to act out the important women, such as:

- Who played her tambourine and sang and danced after she crossed the Reed Sea? (Miriam.)
- Who gave the camels of Avraham's servant, Eliezer, a drink at the well? (Rivka—Rebecca.)
- Who are the sisters that Ya'akov married? (Rachel and Leah.)
- Who laughed when she learned at a very old age that she would give birth to a son? (Sarah.)

Do the same thing with the important men who have been discussed in the Torah so far. See how many the children remember. Who were the important leaders? Discuss what made them good leaders.

Parashat Pinhas Family Discussion

(from *Morah, Morah, Teach Me Torah*)

This parashah is about Pinhas, the son of Eleazar, who was Aharon's sons, and also one of the *kohanim*. In this parashah, Pinhas received a special honor. He becames one of the leaders and helped Moshe and Aharon lead the Israelites into Canaan. Once again the people were counted. Moshe told the people that when they enter Canaan, the land will be divided among the families. In those days only the men were given land. In Parashat Pinhas, there were five daughters of a man named Zelophehad. The daughters came to Moshe and told him that they had no father and no brothers to receive land, but they felt they deserved to be given land to farm. God agreed and Moshe gave them some land. God spoke to Moshe and told him to climb to the top of the mountain so he could see the land of Canaan. Remember because Moshe hit the rock to get water (instead of speaking to it), he would not be allowed to enter Canaan. He is told that Yehoshua (Joshua) will be the next leader of the Israelites and will lead them into Canaan. The people are reminded to celebrate Shabbat, Rosh ha-Shanah, Yom Kippur, Sukkot, Pesah, and Shavuot.

Family Discussion Questions:

1. (Q) Do you think Zelophehad's daughters deserved land?

Try to remember other important women who were mentioned in the Torah.

2. (Q) Who played the tambourine and sang and danced after she crossed the Reed Sea? (A) Miriam.
3. (Q) Who were the sisters that Ya'akov married? (A) Rachel and Leah.
4. (Q) Who gave the cames of Avraham's servant, Eliezer, a drink at the well? (A) Rivka.

MATTOT

We learned about Zelophehad's daughters receiving land in last week's parashah. This week we read Parashat Mattot, which means "tribes." Moshe talks to the heads of the tribes of the Children of Israel. God reminds the Jewish people to keep their promises. It is better NOT to do something than to promise to do it and then break your promise.

The Jewish people went to war against the people of Midian. Moshe's wife Tzipporah was from Midian. After her father Yitro (Jethro) died, the people started doing the wrong things. The people of Midian were trying to get the Jewish people to pray to idols. (Do Jewish people pray to idols? No way!) There was a big war, and the Jewish people won! They returned from battle with lots of clothing and household items from Midian. God told Moshe that anything that was to be used must be thoroughly washed first with boiling water. This is called "kashering" (making things kosher). Many people still do this to household items today.

(Have pots and pans available to act out this parashah and the following song.)

SONG (tune: "This is the Way We Wash Our Clothes"—traditional)

We're gonna wash our pots and pans, pots and pans, pots and pans
We're gonna wash our pots and pans
Gonna kasher the best we can.

Boil the water and scrub them clean, scrub them clean, scrub them clean
Boil the water and scrub them clean
The cleanest pots you've ever seen.

(Repeat first verse)

The Children of Israel are almost in Canaan. They arrive at the Jordan River. It is very beautiful, and the tribes of Gad, Reuven, and some of Menashe like the area very much. They want to stay there.

"It's so beautiful here! There's lots of green grass and large fields for our flocks. We want to stay here east of the Jordan River," said the three tribes to Moshe.

Moshe became angry! "The land of Canaan was promised to our ancestors Avraham [Abraham], Yitzhak [Isaac], and Ya'akov [Jacob]. God took us out of slavery in Egypt and showed us many miracles. We are about to go to war to take the land of Canaan, where God has led us, and YOU want to stay here? Are you meshugah?" replied Moshe. (That means, Are you crazy?)

"Okay. We promise we will go with you and fight alongside our brothers. Then we will return here to live," said the tribes of Gad, Reuven, and some of Menashe.

"All right! If you promise to help, then you can have this land as your own," answered Moshe. "Then you're allowed to stay. But, only if you help us!"

(See song in Multimedia Ideas.)

The Jewish people have wandered in the desert for forty years in order to reach the Promised Land of Canaan. Stay tuned for next week's parashah!

MULTIMEDIA IDEAS

"ASK ME" STICKER: Ask me if it is important to keep promises.

SONG **(tune: "Achshav"—Israeli traditional; try the dance as well!)**

We came upon the Jordan River (2x)
Oh—Reuven, Menashe, and Gad, they wanted to stay—hey
"Are you meshugah?" was all Moshe could say.

We came upon the Jordan River (2x)
Oh—Reuven, Menashe, and Gad, they wanted to stay—hey
"Only if you help us, then you're allowed to stay."

GEOGRAPHY: Take out a map of Israel and see if you can find the Jordan River.

CRAFT: Make a large floor map of Israel (using a large flannel backed tablecloth), and have the children add pictures or other objects for key cities in Israel. Use blocks for the *Kotel* or tall buildings in Tel Aviv, place palm trees and camels in the Negev, etc. Include the Jordan River with a grassy bank.

HOUSEKEEPING: God taught Moshe about making items kosher that they got from Midian. Take out the pots and pans from your family corner and pretend to "kasher" them in the water table. Supply soap and sponges, too.

LANGUAGE: The people of Midian tried to sway the Jewish people into believing in idols. Talk about and record times you were pressured into doing something by your friends. Has anyone ever asked you to do something you knew you should not do? See what examples they come up with, and brainstorm ideas for appropriate responses.

Parashat Mattot Family Discussion

(from *Morah, Morah, Teach Me Torah*)

Mattot means "tribes." Moshe talks to the tribes of Israel. God reminds the people to keep their promises. It is better not to do something than to promise to do it and break your promise.

The Jewish people go to war with the people of Midian. Moshe's wife, Tzipporah, was from Midian. The Jewish people won this war, and when they returned from battle, they brought back many household items. God instructed Moshe that these things were to be thoroughly washed with boiling water before using them. This is called "kashering," making something kosher. Today we can still kasher household items in the same manner.

The Children of Israel are almost in Canaan. They arrive at the Jordan River. It is so beautiful and green there that some of the tribes—Gad, Reuven, and some of the tribe of Menashe—want to stay there. Moshe gets angry. The land of Canaan was promised to their ancestors Avraham, Yitzhak, and Ya'akov (Abraham, Isaac and Jacob). God took the Jews out of slavery and showed them many miracles. They were about to go to war with Canaan. These tribes should help the rest of the people first. Then they could return to live by the Jordan River.

Family Discussion Questions:

1. (Q) Take out a map of Israel and see where the Jordan River is.
2. (Q) Talk about a time when you promised to do something but didn't keep your promise. How did you feel when you broke a promise? How do you think the other person felt?

MAS'EI

Last week we learned about kashering pots and pans and how some of the tribes wanted to stay by the Jordan River. This week, we read Parashat Mas'ei. The word *mas'ei* means "marching." The people of Israel are finally ready to march into the land of Canaan. This parashah is not only important because the Jewish people are finally going to be in *Eretz Yisrael* (the Land of Israel), the land they can call their own, just as God had promised; but it is also important because this is the last parashah of the fourth book of the Torah, the book of Be-Midbar.

The parashah begins by remembering all the places they have traveled since they were freed from being slaves. Do you remember some of the places they went? They were slaves to the mean Pharaoh and were freed from _______________ (Egypt). They came to a big water and they had to cross it and Moshe used his staff to open the ____________ (Reed Sea). They went to the desert wilderness where there was a mountain where they received the Ten Commandments called ______________ (Mount Sinai). And here they are in *Eretz Yisrael*, which at that time was called _____________ (Canaan). They enter into the land by the Jordan River.

(SONG/MOVEMENT (tune: "This Is the Way We Wash Our Clothes"—traditional)

Choose two children to be Pinhas and Yehoshua (Joshua), leading the group in this activity.

This is the way we march along, march along, march along
This is the way we march along, into the land of Canaan.
This is the way we skip along into the land of Canaan.

(Continue with run, hop, gallop etc.)

The land is divided among the people, and God teaches them good rules for living in the Promised Land so the people can live together in peace.

(Show a map of Israel of that time period. There is one available through www.originofnations.org. Click on maps of the migration of Israel.)

Moshe tells the people the boundaries of the land. The city of Edom is to the south, the Mediterranean Sea is to the west, in the north there is a line drawn from Mount Hor to Hazar-enan, and, the land goes along the Jordan River and the Dead Sea on the east.

These are the areas in which they may build their homes.

There is a song in Hebrew that sings about the north, east, south, and west:

SONG (Israeli traditional)

Ufaratzta (4x) *Yamah* (west) *v'kedmah* (east) *tzafonah* (north) *v'negbah* (south—the Negev).

(Label the walls of your room with signs of north, east, west and south in Hebrew and English. As you sing this song, jump to face the appropriate wall.)

This is the last parashah in the book of Be-Midbar. What do we sing when we finish a book of the Torah? "*Hazak, hazak, V'nit-hazek*. Be strong, be strong, and be strenghtened."

SONG (tune: "Mary had a Little Lamb"—traditional)

Hazak, Hazak, v'nit-hazek, v'nit-hazek, v'nit-hazek.
Hazak, Hazak, v'nit-hazek—be brave and be strong.

We read five books of the Torah, the Torah, the Torah.
We read five books of the Torah and then we say *hazak*.

Now we finished Be-Midbar, Be-Midbar, Be-Midbar.
Now we finished Be-Midbar and so we say *hazak*.

Hazak, Hazak, v'nit-hazek, v'nit-hazek, v'nit-hazek.
Hazak, Hazak, v'nit-hazek—be brave and be strong.

MULTIMEDIA IDEAS

"ASK ME" STICKER: Ask me what land the Jewish people were going to enter.

GEOGRAPHY: Laminate a picture of what Israel looked like when it was Canaan. At the same time show a map of Israel as it is to-day to compare then and now.

MOVEMENT: Place a very large map of Israel or an outline of Israel on the floor of your room. To make your own map of Israel have a child lie on the floor on his or her back on butcher pa-per. Have the child bend the right knee and put the right foot on the left knee. Have the child raise the left arm over his or her head, and trace the outline. Add the Dead Sea, the Red Sea, etc. Write signs for the different places the people of Israel traveled through in the appropriate places. Play marching music to march around the room and then to Israel.

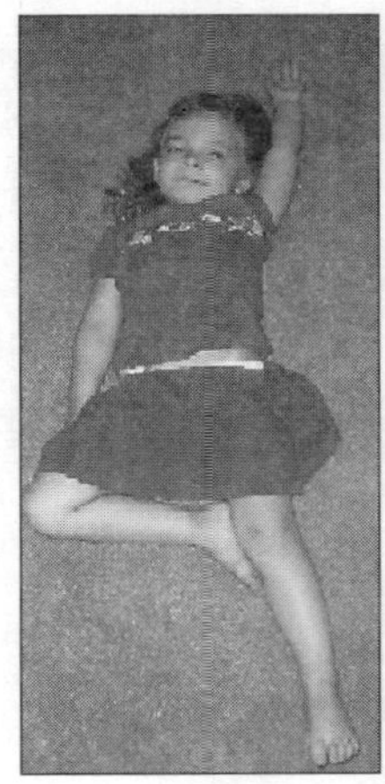

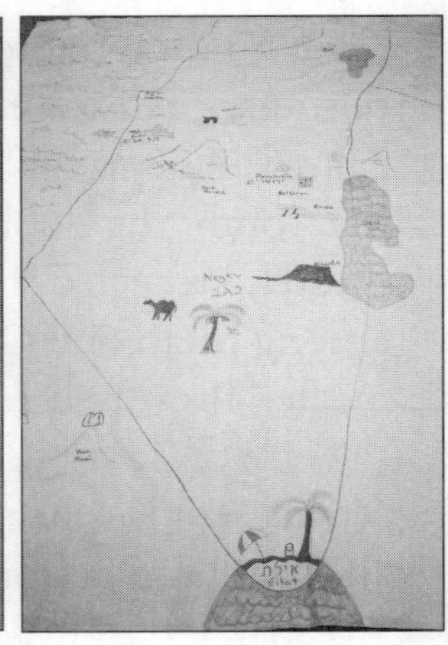

CRAFT: Draw pictures of the different places the Jewish people went: Mount Sinai, the Reed Sea, the desert, etc.

MATH: It's a good time to look at maps and perhaps create a map. It could be a map of your school or of your town. Post a map of the United States and of Israel. Have the children tell you which cities or states they have relatives living, and mark them with colored pushpins.

CRAFT: Make a *Mizra<u>h</u>*. When Jewish people (in the Diaspora) pray, they face east toward Israel—toward Jerusalem. In Hebrew mizra<u>h</u> means "east." Out of felt or fabric, write the word *MIZRA<u>H</u>* in Hebrew מזרח (*mem-zayin-resh-<u>h</u>et*; remember to write it from right to left) or in English. Decorate it any way you like, such as with the Jerusalem skyline, Magen David, flowers, etc.

Parashat Mas'ei Family Discussion

(from *Morah, Morah, Teach Me Torah*)

The word Mas'ei means "marching." The people of Israel are finally ready to march into the land of Canaan. This parashah is not only important because *B'nai Yisrael* were finally going to be in a land they could call their own, but this is also the last parashah in the fourth book of the Torah, the book of Be-Midbar. The parashah reviews all the places they had traveled since they were slaves in Egypt. The land was divided among them and God taught the people good rules for living in peace in the "Promised Land." Moshe tells them the boundaries of the land: the city of Edom to the south, the Mediterranean Sea to the west, from Mount Hor to Hazar-enan on the north, and land along the Jordan River and the Dead Sea on the east.

Family Discussion Questions:

1. (Q) Can you name some of the places the Jews traveled through? (A) They left Egypt from slavery, they crossed the Reed Sea, they wandered in the wilderness/desert, they came to Mount Sinai in the desert where they received the Ten Commandments, they reached the Jordan River.
2. (Q) Look at a map of Israel and see if you can find some of these places where *B'nai Yisrael* traveled.
3. (Q) What do we say when we finish reading one of the books of the Torah? (A) *Hazak, hazak v'nit-hazek*—be strong and be strengthened.
4. Since the people are about to enter into the Land of Israel, sing some Israeli songs together.

INTRODUCTION TO DEVARIM

Notes for Teachers

Because much of the book of Devarim repeats the importance of remembering the laws for the Jewish people, the Ten Commandments, the laws of kashrut, and other laws, some of the ideas, songs, and activities may be repetitive of those mentioned in earlier parashiyot. But we always explain to the children that for any really great book, we want to hear it and read it over and over again. The Torah is the greatest book; we read and reread it every year!

For most teachers, the school year is beginning now, with the last book of the Torah. WAIT, we're starting at the end? There's NEVER an end to studying Torah. It is also a great time to review the five books and explain that every year, at Simhat Torah, we begin again. So, let's see what they remember. Perhaps make it a game!

SONG (tune: Adon Olam—traditional, the repetitive version)

Oh there are five [shout out "five" and put out your hand] books of the Torah
Oh there are five (five) books that we read
Oh there are five (five) books of the Torah
We read five books of Torah each and every year.

First is BERESHIT, then we read SHEMOT
And then we read the book of VA-YIKRA
Then comes BE-MIDBAR, and last is DEVARIM
And then we start all over and we read it again.

Oh there are five (five) books of the Torah
Oh there five (five) books that we read
Oh there five (five) books of the Torah
We read five books of Torah each and every year.

(If you want to make it a game, break your class or group into five groups representing the "Five Books," act out ideas from each book, and have the children guess which book is being represented.

SUMMARY GAME: The Bereshit group can act out or show pictures depicting events that occurred in this book, for example, a globe to represent creation of the world, Adam and Eve (*Hava*) and the snake, Noah and the ark, etc. The name of the first book in the Torah is Bereshit. *Bereshit* means "in the beginning" (seems like a good place to start!). This book tells how God made the world.

Next have the children act as slaves, Moshe, and Pharaoh. The second book is called Shemot. This book explains how the Jewish people became slaves and had to work very hard in Egypt. God took them out of slavery and gave them the Ten Commandments.

Next, children can bring gifts to the *Mishkan*. The third book is Va-Yikra. It teaches the Jewish people lots of laws and about gift offerings to God. We also learn all about the *Mishkan*.

Next, show pictures of the tribes and have the children pretend to walk in the desert for forty years. The fourth book is Be-Midbar. Be-Midbar means "in the desert/wilderness." We learn all about counting the Jewish people and what happens while they are wandering in the desert.

And last, you can have Moshe hand over the Torah to Yehoshua and the children pretend to enter the Promised Land. The fifth book is called Devarim. *Devarim* means "the words." In this book we hear a lot of the laws repeated and learn what Moshe needs to teach the Jewish people before he dies and before they enter the land of Canaan.

DEVARIM

The parashah Devarim is the first parashah in the fifth (and last) book of the Torah. *B'nai Yisrael* (the Jewish people) are camped across the Jordan River from Canaan. For forty years they have traveled in the desert. A whole new generation of people have been born and grown up in the desert. Only Moshe, Yehoshua (Joshua), and Caleb remain from the original people who were freed from slavery in Egypt.

Devarim means "the words." so these are the words of God as told to Moshe. Moshe gathers the people and reminds them of all the times that they lost faith in God. Moshe names all the places where the Jewish people were when they didn't follow God's laws. Moshe reminds the people to follow the Torah and to follow God's laws: Try to judge people fairly, don't complain, and have trust in God. Remember not to do things you aren't supposed to do. Only do what God wants us to do. Moshe speaks for thirty-six days! He tries to teach a very important lesson. Everyone makes mistakes, but we must learn from our mistakes, and do *t'shuvah* (say "I'm sorry").

Moshe then makes Yehoshua (Joshua) the new leader of the Jewish people because Moshe will not enter the land of Canaan., (Remember when he hit the rock instead of speaking to it? See Parashat Hukkat.) Moshe is 120 years old and knows he will die soon.

MULTIMEDIA IDEAS

"ASK ME" STICKER: Ask me about one of the important rules the Jewish people should follow.

SONG **(traditional Israeli folk song)**
This is a nice song for using the ASL signs also.

Al sh'loshah d'varim, al sh'loshah d'varim,
al sh'loshah sh'loshah d'varim ha-olam, ha-olam omed.
Al ha-Torah, v'al ha-avodah, v'al g'milut hasadim.
Al ha-Torah, v'al ha-avodah, v'al g'milut hasadim.

On three words (2x)
On three, three words, the world, the world stands.
On the Torah, and on prayer, and on good deeds throughout the land. (2x)

LANGUAGE: Discuss *g'milut hasadim* (acts of kindness). What are acts of kindness? How can we do them? Make a list and post them in the classroom.

TZEDAKAH: Practice acts of *hesed* (kindness) by doing a *tzedakah* project. Visit a nursing home with your children (sing songs!) or invite seniors to visit you. Make cards or packages (kosher) for Israeli soldiers. Brainstorm with your kids ideas that they would like to do.

GAME: Moshe appoints a new leader. Play "Moshe, Moshe, Yehoshua" (like "Duck, Duck, Goose").

MATH: We talk about wandering in the desert for forty years. The number forty has been used before. Can you remember when? (It rained for forty days and nights in Parashat Noah, and Moshe was on Har Sinai for forty days and nights.) Can you count to forty? Make four groups of ten?

Parashat Devarim Family Discussion

(from *Morah, Morah, Teach Me Torah*)

We begin reading the last book of the Torah, Devarim. This book of the Torah is usually read near the beginning of the school year. Isn't it amazing that we are starting school at the end of the Torah? But, like all really great books, we like to read them over and over again. *Devarim* means "words," so these are God's words that Moshe tells the people. They are reminded of all the times they lost faith in God. The people are camped across the Jordan River waiting to go into Canaan. For forty years they have wandered in the desert. Only two people from the people freed from slavery will enter Canaan, Yehoshua and Caleb. Moshe reminds the people to follow the Torah and its laws, to judge people fairly, and to learn from their mistakes. Moshe speaks for thirty-six days. Because Moshe cannot enter the land of Canaan (remember when he hit the rock to get water instead of speaking to it as God instructed?), God has him appoint Yehoshua to be the new leader of the Jewish people and to lead them into Canaan.

Family Discussion Questions:

1. (Q) *Devarim* means "the words." Whose words are the people listening to? (A) God's words through Moshe.
2. (Q) How many years did the Jewish people wander in the desert? (A) Forty.
3. (Q) God told the people to treat people fairly. What are some ways you could treat people fairly?

VA-ETHANNAN

Last week we began the book Devarim. This week we read Parashat Va'Ethannan, which means "and I pleaded." This parashah begins with Moshe pleading with God to allow him to enter the land of Canaan. God punished Moshe (do you remember why?). He was punished for hitting the rock, and God would not go back on that punishment. (see Parashat Hukkat). Moshe had to live with the consequences of his actions. It was Moshe's job to prepare Yehoshua to lead the people. "Follow the rules of the Torah and you will have a good life."

It is written in the Torah that "the words and blessings of God shall be upon your heart and upon your soul; you shall bind them as a sign upon your arm and between your eyes. You shall write them on the doorposts of your house and upon your gates." This is part of the Shema prayer, which we say when we wake up in the morning and when we go to sleep at night. Hold up your right hand and sing:

SONG (tune: Here We Go 'Round the Mulberry Bush—traditional)

Where oh where is your right hand, your right hand, your right hand?
Where oh where is your right hand, we need it for the Shema.

(Let's say the Shema together.)

שְׁמַע יִשְׂרָאֵל יי אֱלֹהֵינוּ יי אֶחָד.

Shema Yisrael Adonai Eloheinu Adonai Ehad.
Listen, Israel, the Eternal is our God, the Eternal is One.

We should remember these words always, and to help us remember them, there are two places where these words can be found:

(1) They are written inside *tefillin*. Many men (and some women) wear *tefillin* when they pray.

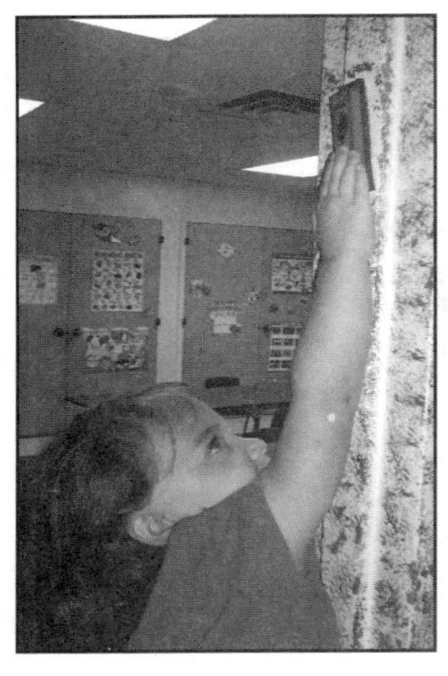

They wrap part of the strap around their arm, and the other part goes on their forehead.

(2) A mezuzah has God's special prayer inside. Who knows where we can find a mezuzah? It's on the doorpost of your house, and we can also find it on the doorpost of our synagogue. The Hebrew letter שׁ *shin* is written on both the mezuzah and the *tefillin*. The *shin* is a symbol for God's name. Let's go and find the mezuzah, look for the *shin*. Do you remember why we have a mezuzah? We learned about it in Parashat Bo.

MULTIMEDIA IDEAS

"ASK ME" STICKERS: Ask me to say the Shema.

CRAFT: 1) Make a mezuzah. There are many ways to make a mezuzah. One way is to use a piece of bamboo (if you cut it below the knot, you have a plug for the bottom—a plug for the top can be purchased at a craft store), or you can use wood 3/4 round (a corner wall molding), or you could use recycled fax paper rolls. Cut and decorate them using tissue paper and watered-down glue, or paint them. Write the Shema on a small piece of paper, roll it up and put it inside the mezuzah. Or contact your rabbi to purchase a kosher parchment.

OR

Make a mezuzah. There are wonderful kits available from Just for the Mitzvah (888-4 THE MIT) and Kosher Krafts (800-957-2387).

2) Ask children to bring in a mezuzah, or show some mezuzot to show how different they can look. They may all look different from the outside, but they are alike on the inside because they have the same prayer inside.

SONG "I Have a Mezuzah" by Uncle Moishe, Volume I (tune: "Where is Thumbkin")

I have a mezuzah (repeat)
On my door (repeat)
Now I will tell you (repeat)
What it's for (repeat).

I protect you (repeat)
Day and night (repeat)
As you enter (repeat)
I'm on your right (repeat)

To kiss the mezuzah (repeat)
Is our aim (repeat)
For on it is written (repeat)
Hashem's name (repeat).

Parashat Va-Ethannan Family Discussion

(from *Morah, Morah, Teach Me Torah*)

Va-ethannan means "and I pleaded." This parashah begins with Moshe pleading with God to allow him to enter the land of Canaan. But God stays true to the punishment. Now Moshe's job was to prepare Yehoshua (Joshua) to lead the people. It is written in the Torah that "the words and blessings of God shall be upon your heart and upon your soul; you shall bind them as a sign upon your arm and between your eyes. You shall write them on the doorposts of your house and upon your gates." This is part of the Shema prayer, which we say when we wake up in the morning and when we go to sleep at night. These words are also written on the *tefillin* that many men (and some women) wear when they pray as they wrap the straps around part of their arm and between their eyes. A mezuzah also has the same prayer inside it. Where do we put a mezuzah? We will find it on the doorposts of our homes, our rooms, and in our synagogues.

Family Discussion Questions:

1. See if you can say the Shema prayer together.
2. Look for mezuzot at your house and other Jewish buildings, such as the synagogue.
3. Do you think that Moshe should be allowed to enter the Promised Land? Why, or why not?

EKEV

Last week we learned about the prayer the Shema and why we have a mezuzah.

This week we read Parashat Ekev, which means "rewards"—what can happen if the people remember the rules that Moshe teaches. Moshe reviewed the experiences that the Israelites had in the desert. He reminded them of all the hardships that happened and the good things that happened.

Moshe also reminded the people, "Remember when I came down from *Har Sinai* and found you praying to the golden calf? I had to go all the way back up the mountain again. Never, never let this happen again."

Moshe wanted the Jewish people to understand that if they do all that God asked them to do and they follow the commandments, then their lives would be pleasant and good for them.

Moshe said to the people, "God will bless you, and you will have lots of children, and God will remove sickness. Remember, God took you out of slavery in Egypt. God fed you manna so you wouldn't starve. God made sure that your clothes and your shoes wouldn't become worn out while you were traveling through the desert. Now God brought you to this wonderful land, flowing with milk and honey, with hills and streams; a land filled with wheat and barley, dates, figs, grapes and pomegranates, and olives. (Have samples of the seven species or pictures of them for the children to see.)

These special foods are called the "seven species" and they are important because they grow in *Eretz Yisrael* (Israel). They were the fruits and grain that the Israelites first found when they entered the land. The Torah commanded every farmer to bring the first fruits and grain harvests as an offering to God (*bikkurim*).

SONG (tune: "Supercalifragilistic," music by Richard M. Sherman with adaptations by the authors)

Wheat, grapes, barley, olives, dates and figs and pomegranates
Yummy grains and fruits that grow, they all taste fantastic
There are seven species that grow in *Yisrael*
Wheat, grapes, barley, olives, dates, and figs and pomegranates
Yum diddle, diddle, diddle yum diddle di.

After we have eaten the good foods, there is a prayer that we can say to thank God for all the food we have. It's called the *Birkat ha-Mazon*. God commanded the Jewish people to say thank You to God after finishing eating. "And you shall eat and you shall be satisfied. And you shall bless God, for the good land given to you."

MULTIMEDIA IDEAS

"ASK ME" STICKER: Ask me about all the yummy foods that grow in Israel.

SCIENCE/COOKING: Make barley soup Add barley to the vegetable soup recipe in Parashat Toldot (page 53).

(1) Look at raw wheat and barley.

(2) Buy two each of the following fruits: pomegranates, dates, figs, olives, and grapes. Without the children, cut open one of each and remove the seeds. Show the children the seeds, and have them predict which seeds go with which fruit. Then look at the inside of each fruit and compare the seeds. If possible, have a photo of the bushes and trees they grow on (posters available at www.tjssc.com or 800-984-3616).

(3) Guess how each fruit will taste (isweet, sour, etc.). Then have a tasting party.

DRAMATIC PLAY: Set up a farmers market (or *shuk*) in your family corner. Have a variety of fruits and vegetables, etc., available. Include price tags, a cash register, and play money to purchase the foods, and have scales to weigh the foods. Make sure you have some *shekelim* to use as well! (*Shekelim* are available at the website above.)

LANGUAGE: Learn *Birkat ha-Mazon* in English or Hebrew. Here is one of the important lines in *Birkat ha-Mazon* (reciting this blessing is also called *benching):*

Barukh Attah Adonai ḫa-zan et ha-kol.

Blessed are You, God who nourishes all.

See the CD *Shlock Rock for Kids Party Time!* for the song "Don't Forget to Bench" (www.shlockrock.com).

SONG: tune: Oh Do You Know the Muffin Man?—traditional

There are seven species in *Yisrael*, in *Yisrael*
There are seven species in *Eretz Yisrael*
Pomegranates, figs, and dates,
Barley, wheat, olives, grapes,
The seven species taste so great,
They grow in *Yisrael.*

There are seven species in *Yisrael*, in *Yisrael*
There are seven species in *Eretz Yisrael.*

Parashat Ekev Family Discussion

(from *Morah, Morah, Teach Me Torah*)

Ekev means "a reward." Moshe told the Jewish people their reward if they remember and follow all the laws that God taught them. Moshe reminded them of all the hardships that happened on their journey and the good things that happened. *B'nai Yisrael* had to learn from what they had done. If they do this, God will reward them. Remember how God made sure the Children of Israel had food to eat (manna and quail), so they wouldn't starve, and water to drink, and God brought them to a land filled with wheat and barley, dates, figs, grapes, pomegranates, and olives. These foods are the "seven species," and they are important because these are the foods that grow in Israel. The Torah commanded every farmer to bring the first fruits and first harvests as an offering to God (*bikkurim*). After we eat good foods, there is a special prayer we recite to say thank you to God for the food we have; it's called *Birkat ha-Mazon*. It tells us in the Torah,"...And you shall eat and you shall be satisfied. And you shall bless God for the good land given to you. Amen!"

Family Discussion Questions:

1. (Q) At home, when you do the things that you should, how might your mom and dad reward you?
2. (Q) Can you name the "seven species" of Israel? (A) Olives, grapes, pomegranates, wheat, barley, figs, and dates.
3. (Q) Did you have any of the seven species in your Shabbat dinner? (A) Hallah is made from wheat; maybe a salad with olives or pomegranates?
4. After dinner, try to say *Birkat ha-Mazon.* It is found in a siddur or *bencher.*

RE'EH

Last week we learned about the seven species and the blessing we recite after a meal to thank God for all the food we have.

This week we read Parashat Re'eh, which means "to see." We learn that Moshe told the Israelites that everyone had choices to make in the way they behave. If they behave well, they would be blessed; if they choose to behave badly and not follow the laws, they would be cursed or punished. The same is still true for us today. We can choose to follow the rules and laws or to disobey them. If you do what your teacher or parents ask you to do, how do you feel? How does your teacher or parents feel? What if you **don't** obey them, how do they feel? You will see that God will present the people with a blessing or a curse.

Moshe told the people to watch out for those who would try to persuade them to do something they think is wrong. For instance, if a person said to them, "Look at this beautiful idol. If you say a prayer to this statue, you will be rich, and your plants will grow fast." Should the people do this? If your heart tells you NO, then do what you FEEL and KNOW is right. There are Hebrew words that carry this meaning. If you feel that something is right and good, we say it's your *yetzer ha-tov*. Do you remember what the word *tov* means? (Good!) If you feel, in your heart that something is wrong, we say it's your *yetzer ha-ra*.

(Have children show the kind of face that represents each verse—happy face for *yetzer ha-tov* and sad face for *yetzer ha-ra*. You could even have them make props with the icons ☺ and ☹.)

SONG (tune: "Three Blind Mice"—traditional)

☹

Yetzer ha-ra, Yetzer ha-ra
That's when I do things BAD (2x)
Yetzer ha-ra is when I choose
To do things that are mean and rude
And sometimes I have a bad attitude
Yetzer ha-ra, Yetzer ha-ra.

☺

Yetzer ha-tov, Yetzer ha-tov
I do things that are GOOD (2x)
Yetzer ha-tov, I choose to be kind
I try to think with others in mind
I try not to leave any friends behind
Yetzer ha-tov, Yetzer ha-tov.

God told the Jewish people that they were special ("The chosen people") and to remember that they were different from the other nations. They should try not to copy the bad behavior of other people.

Again they were reminded to share what they had. If a poor person has borrowed money from you and you wait and wait for them to pay it back, but still they can't pay it back, don't embarrass them and ask for it. It will make you a better person if you just feel like you gave the money to someone who needed it and you have helped that person out. If feels good to give; it's called giving *Tzedakah*. The Hebrew word for a righteous person is "a *tzaddik*."

MULTIMEDIA IDEAS

"ASK ME" STICKERS: Ask me what makes me special. Ask me about using my *Yetzer ha-Tov.*

SONG (tune: "B-I-N-G-O"—graditional)

God gave us lots of special gifts that we must share with others.
S-H-A-R-E (3x)
We share all that we have.

(You can take paper and make the letters S H A R E to hold up for visual cues while singing the song.)

DRAMATIC PLAY: Have children act out/role-play various situations of "right" and "wrong," such as:

1) You find your friend's favorite toy left behind at school. What should you do? Should you keep the toy and say, "Finders keepers, losers weepers"?

2) Your mom has made you a big batch of your favorite chocolate chip cookies. You have friends playing at your house. You really want to eat all those cookies yourself. Should you eat them in front of your friends and not give them any, or should you share them equally with them?

(*The Doorbell Rang* by Pat Hutchins is about sharing cookies equally with friends. This book is not only a good one for acting out, but it's a great MATH experience as well.)

3) Your friend gets hurt on the playground and is crying. You're busying playing somewhere else at the time. What should you do?—stop what you're doing and go over to your friend to help, or just continue playing where you were?

CRAFT: Draw pictures or find pictures of people helping others, doing good deeds, and doing mean or unkind things.

LANGUAGE: Talk about what happens in school or at home when you don't listen and follow rules. Record the ideas. For example, some children get time-out, have to sit on the steps, or go to their rooms, etc.

MATH: Make a graph or Venn diagram of the "punishments" to see how many get time-out, how many have to go to their rooms, etc.

Because we talk about how being Jewish makes us special and unique, try this ACTIVITY:

A JEWISH SCAVENGER HUNT: Hide a variety of Jewish items, things that make us different and special, around the room, school or home and find them. Items can include *tzedakah* box, kiddush cup, *kippah*, spice box, *Havdalah* candle, Shabbat candlesticks, *hallah* cover, shofar. You can also hide pictures of any items you don't have.

BOOKS: These books have a sharing theme:

1) *Tikum Olam: Fixing the World* by Anne Lobock Fenton

2) *Rabbi Chanina and the Beautiful Brown Hen*, part of Jewish legends and stories for parents and children—a program designed by Dvora Lifshitz and Ofra Reisman

GAME: Using Google Images, find pictures of different activities that are kind and pictures of activities that are not kind. Make two sets and use as a lotto game or sort into categories, such as kindness versus not kind, or kindness toward people versus kindness to the land, etc. Examples might include throwing trash in the trash cans, helping a friend, sharing toys, etc.

Re'eh Family Discussion

(from *Morah, Morah, Teach Me Torah*)

This week in Parashat Re'eh (which means "to see"), we learn that everyone has a choice to make in the way they behave. If they behave well (*yetzer ha-tov*), God will bless them. If they choose to behave unkindly (*yetzer ha-ra*) and not follow the laws, then they will be punished. We talked a lot about *yetzer ha-tov* and *yetzer ha-ra*. (Remember that *tov* means "good!")

Moshe told the people to watch out for people who try to tell them to do something they know they shouldn't do (peer pressure). They have to listen to their hearts and follow the rules. They have to remember that they are special and different from the other nations. They must not copy other people's bad behavior.

They are also reminded to share all that they have with others, and to give *tzedakah*.

Family Discussion Questions:

1. (Q) Between *yetzer ha-ra* and *yetzer ha-tov*, which one means to be good?
2. (Q) Do you think you have a choice whether to be good and kind, or not?
3. (Q) What do you think it means to be the chosen people? (A) Remember that on Mount Sinai when the people were about to receive the Ten Commandments, they said "All that God says, we will do," even before they knew what the rules were.
4. (Q) Why is *tzedakah* so important? (A) It is an obligation, not a choice.

SHOFTIM

Last week we talked about *yetzer ha-ra* and *yetzer ha-tov*. Do you remember which one means being good?

In Parashat Shoftim, Moshe was still teaching the Jewish people the laws they should follow before entering Canaan. *Shoftim* are the judges. Moshe taught that there must be judges to help people. The judges must be fair! They shouldn't rule in favor of their friends, only in favor of who is right. It is written in the Torah "*Tzedek, tzedek tirdof.* Justice, justice you shall pursue." Do you remember what the word *tzaddik* means? (A holy person who does what is right.)

Moshe also instructed *B'nai Yisrael* about the mitzvah *bal tash'hit*—not being wasteful, preserving the earth.

SONG (tune: "Twinkle, Twinkle Little Star"—traditional)

Everybody must be fair, everyone must show they care.
Don't be wasteful, please be kind.
Try to think with others in mind.
Everybody must be fair, everyone must show they care.

Moshe then taught that kings must also be fair. They couldn't own too much, only what they need. The parashah tells us that kings had to have their own Torahs. They had to learn from the Torah and teach others as well. It is also a mitzvah to write, or help to write your own Torah.

Moshe instructed the people about getting ready for war. Moshe told them "When you prepare for war, you must always try to make peace first. And only if things can't be worked out, then you go to war as a last choice. The Jewish people can not cut down any trees that give us food; even if it will help us win the war, you may not cut any down." (Remember *bal tash'hit*! Don't be wasteful!)

MULTIMEDIA IDEAS

"ASK ME" STICKER: Ask me how to not be wasteful.

GAME: Play a game where you figure out what fruits grow on trees in Israel and what fruits grow on trees where students live. Are there any that are the same?

Home	Israel
apples, oranges, peaches	pomegranates,
plums, pears	olives, figs, dates
oranges, lemons	oranges, lemons

Write/draw cards for each fruit and have the children place them in the right category. How many grow in both places?

SCIENCE/MATH: We learned about judges weighing fairly. Practice weighing things with a scale. Can you make both sides of the scale even?

LANGUAGE: We learned about *bal tash'hit* (not being wasteful). Talk about ways we can avoid being wasteful (e.g., shutting off lights/TV when we are not in the room, not running the water when we brush our teeth.)

BOOK: *Green Chagim* is a book with craft ideas for the Jewish holidays using recycled products. Find it at www.Torah4kids.com.

CRAFT: We learned that a king must have his own Torah and that it is a mitzvah to write or help to write your own Torah. Use a feather (a large one) and black paint, and try writing like a *sofer* (scribe) who writes a Torah. Go to www.kidstorah.org for information on how to buy a letter in a Torah scroll in Israel for only $1.00.

SONG "The Green Song" by Lenny Solomon, from the CD *Shlock Rock for Kids Party Time!*

The heavens belongs to God but
He gave the earth to man
So we must take good care not to destroy it
Tikkun olam we can complete
If we all clean up our street
This will keep our world going strong.

Chorus: Reuse, recycle, don't litter, don't waste
Bal Tash'hit comes right from the Torah
This is a lesson that we must learn with haste
Ask your rabbi, teacher, or *morah.*

God said to Adam
I created this world for you.
Be careful then that you do not spoil it
For if you don't take care
And leave it in disrepair
No one after you will be able to use it.

BOOK: *Sofer: The Story of a Torah Scroll* by Eric Ray

A *sofer* (Rabbi Dovid Krautwirth) checking some *tefillin* (Dovid88@hotmail.com).

Parashat Shoftim Family Discussion

(from *Morah, Morah, Teach Me Torah*)

Moshe was still teaching the laws to the Jewish people. *Shoftim* were the judges. Moshe taught that there must be judges to help people, and the judges must be fair. It is written in the Torah, "Justice, justice you shall pursue." A king or other leader must be fair to the people, too. Moshe also teaches about the mitzvah of *bal tash'hit*, which means not destroying the earth, not being wasteful. We should not cut down trees that give us food. We are taught to learn from the Torah and teach others as well. That's what we are doing together each week!

Family Discussion Questions:

1. (Q) We learned about not being wasteful. What things can we do to avoid being wasteful at home? (A) Turn off lights and water so we don't waste it, recycle items that can be recycled, etc.
2. (Q) Talk about a time when there was something you thought was not fair.
3. (Q) What is the Hebrew word that means "judges"? (A) Shoftim.

KI TETZE

Last week we learned that judges must be fair and that kings must be fair. In this week's parashah, Ki Tetze, which means "when you go out," Moshe instructs the Jewish people that all people, even parents and children must be fair. Parents need to be fair to all their children; they cannot choose one over the others, or have favorites. (Do you remember Ya'akov's favorite son? He had a coat with many colors. Yosef!) Children must be fair too and obey their teachers and parents.

Then Moshe taught about being kind. He told the Jewish people to remember the mitzvah *hashovat aveidah*—returning lost things. If we find something that isn't ours, what should we do? We must try very hard to find its owners.

SONG: "*Hashovas Aveidah*" by Zale Newman, from the CD Uncle Moishe, Volume 3

Hashovas aveidah, this is what it means,
Hashovas aveidah, means returning those lost things.
Hashovas aveidah, don't just turn away,
Hashovas aveidah, means return them right away.

If we see an animal that is hurt or lost we must help it. That is the mitzvah of *tza'ar ba'alei hayyim*—compassion to animals. If we work on a farm, we are not allowed to work two animals that are not equal to each other. (For example, we can't have one ox and one small pony trying to pull something at the same time. The ox is much stronger, and it is not fair to the small pony.)

(To show an example of this, have an adult and a child play tug of war or arm wrestle. Are the teams evenly matched? Is this fair?)

We must also share all that we have with others who are less fortunate than we are. We must share our crops in the fields, our food, and our money with those in need. We are commanded to leave the corners of our fields for the poor. (Remember the song "S-H-A-R-E" in Parashat Terumah?)

We are also reminded not to say unkind words to others. It hurts their feelings to speak *lashon ha-ra*. We are not allowed to hurt people deliberately.

SONG (tune: "Three Blind Mice"—traditional)

Say kind words, say kind words
Don't speak *lashon ha-ra* (2x)
Always think about what you say
Our words can hurt people, that's not okay
If you're wrong, say you're sorry right away.
Say kind words!

MULTIMEDIA IDEAS

"ASK ME" STICKER: Ask me what I should do if I find a lost item. It's the mitzvah *hashovat aveidah*.

BOOK: Read *Yettele's Feathers* by Joan Rothenberg. It's a story about a woman who gossips and says unkind things about people in the town. See what happens when she begins to offend the townspeople. (It's also fun to act out!)

GAME: Moshe reminded us to return lost things. Play the game "Doggie, doggie where's your bone?"

DRAMATIC PLAY/GAME: We learned about sharing our food and our crops with others. Take your play food and act out leaving the corners of your fields for others (gleaning) and sharing food. Set up a restaurant too. (The book of Ruth is a great story to read on this theme.)

GAME: With the play food, play a "What's missing?" game. Take five or six foods and then hide one. Can the kids see what's missing? Or put them in a pillowcase and play a feeling game to guess what's missing.

CRAFT/LANGUAGE: Talk about being kind to animals. Brainstorm ways to be kind to animals. Make animal puppets or masks and play the following game.

GAME: "Hickory dickory dock, the *akhbar* [mouse—add other animals names in Hebrew] went up the clock. The clock struck one and down he run. Hickory dickory dock." The children stand on one side of the room.

They are the animals. Perhaps they can use animal masks or puppets. One person is on the opposite side of the room—the clock who says "hickory dickory dock..." and names an animal to come across the room (running up the clock). To run down the clock, the animals run back to their side of the room.

Horse	*Soos*	סוּס
Duck	*Barvaz*	בַּרְוָז
Cow	*Parah*	פָּרָה
Dog	*Kelev*	כֶּלֶב
Cat	*<u>H</u>atool*	חָתוּל
Pig	*<u>H</u>azir*	חֲזִיר

Parashat Ki Tetze Family Discussion

(from *Morah, Morah, Teach Me Torah*)

This parashah continues talking about being fair. Moshe instructs the Jewish people that all people, not just leaders, should be fair; parents and children need to treat each other fairly too. He teaches us that it is a mitzvah to be kind. He teaches us about *hashovat aveidah*, the mitzvah of returning lost things. If we find something that does not belong to us, what should we do? We should return it to its owner or at least try very hard to find the owner. We learn about the mitzvah of *tza'ar ba'alei h̲ayyim*—compassion to animals, caring and being kind to animals. Once again we are reminded to share what we have, to say kind words to each other, and not to hurt another person deliberately.

Family Discussion Questions:

1. (Q) What kinds of things could you share with others?
2. (Q) Do you remember a story in the Torah where there was an "unfair" situation that made a lot of brothers jealous? Do you remember Yosef (Joseph) and his coat of many colors that his father Ya'akov gave to only to him, and how Ya'akov treated Yosef differently than he treated his other sons? Was that fair? How did Yosef's brothers feel?
3. (Q) If you found a bracelet or money in your classroom, should you just keep it and say, "Finders keepers, losers weepers?" Why or why not? How would you feel if you lost a favorite toy and someone returned it to you?

KI TAVO

Last week we learned about being fair to others and to say kind words.

This week we read Parashat Ki Tavo. Ki Tavo means "when you enter," like when the Jewish people enter the Promised Land. Moshe told the people what they should do when they cross the Jordan River and enter the land of Israel for the first time. Remember, Moshe was still not allowed to go with them because he was being punished for hitting the rock in the desert to get water instead of talking to it (see Parashat H̲ukkat). So Moshe wanted to make sure they will remember all the rules, because he wouldn't be there to remind them once they enter the land.

We keep hearing Moshe telling the people the rules and commandments over and over again. These are all the things they need to know to live in the new land. Only Moshe heared the voice of God who told Moshe what God wants the people to remember.

Moshe told the people to offer the first fruits picked in the Promised Land as a gift offering (*bikkurim*). The first fruits are the most special. Then they talked about all that has happened since the very beginning. Let's see how many things we can remember:

1) Where were the Jewish people living when they were slaves? (Egypt.)
2) Who lead them out of slavery? (Moshe.)
3) Where did Moshe go to get the Ten Commandments? (Har Sinai.)
4) What food did God provide the people in the desert? (Manna.)
5) In what special place did the *Kohein Gadol* keep the laws? (In the ark in the *Mishkan*.)

Moshe particularly wants everyone to remember what will happen if they do good deeds and what will happen if they don't follow the rules. This is what Moshe did:

He gathered the twelve tribes together and divided them into two groups. One group of six would stand on top of *Har Grizim* (Mount Grizim), and one group of six would stand on top of *Har Eval* (Mount Eval).

The group on Mount Grizim would listen for the blessings, or the **tov** (good) deeds to be announced and after each blessing they would hear, they would say "Amen". The group on Mount Eval would listen for the curses, or the **lo tov** (not good) things that they could get punished, for to be announced. (See the list in Multimedia Ideas.)

MULTIMEDIA IDEAS

"ASK ME" STICKER: Ask me if it is important to do good deeds.

SONG **(tune: "The Green Grass Grows All Around"—traditional)**

Oh when you enter (echo)
The Promised Land (echo)
The things you'll do, is follow the rules

Chorus: And, it's very important to do good deeds
And God will bless us all, us all
And God will bless us all.

There were two groups (echo)
Of the twelve tribes (echo).
On Har Grizim and Har Eval.

(Chorus)

On Mount Grizim (echo)
They heard blessings (echo)
On Mount Eval they heard curses.

(Chorus)

DRAMATIC PLAY/LANGUAGE: Divide the class into two groups. Stand on opposite sides of the room, representing the two mountains: Mount Grizim and Mount Eval.

Provide the children on Mount Grizim with happy faces (have the children say *TOV* [good] and do thumbs up) and those on Mount Eval (have the children say *LO TOV* [not good] with sad faces or do thumbs down). Now read a selection of "*Tov*" and "*Lo Tov*" ideas (see below) and they will decide what the appropriate response will be. When you read them, mix them up.

***TOV*—Good**

Someone who returns a lost item.
Someone who helps someone when they fall down.
Someone who shares what they have with others.
Someone who does what their parents or teachers ask them to do.

***LO TOV*—Not Good**

Someone who prays to idols.
Someone who is rude and mean to their parents.
Someone who cheats a stranger or someone who has less than they do.
Someone who steals from another person.

MATH: Since the twelve tribes were divided into two groups, experiment with different ways you can divide twelve things or twelve people into equal groups: three groups of four, four groups of three, or two groups of six. Use the students themselves or have twelve counting things available to have the students make equal groups.

LANGUAGE: This parashah talks about giving the first fruits as an offering (*bikkurim*). Talk about and write down important firsts in the children's lives and in the story of the Jewish people and make a chart:

For example:

THEIR LIVES	HISTORY
first day of school	first day of creation
first tooth lost	first Jew (Avraham)
first trip they remember taking	first people (Adam and Eve [Hava])
first word they spoke	first commandment (I am the Eternal your God)

COOKING: In this parashah God instructed us to offer the first fruits as a gift offering. Make fruit salad and learn the Hebrew names of the fruits. Remember to make the *brakhah* on fruits:

בָּרוּךְ אַתָּה יי אֱלֹהֵינוּ מֶלֶךְ הָעוֹלָם בּוֹרֵא פְּרִי הָאֲדָמָה.

Barukh Attah Adonai, Eloheinu Melekh ha-Olam Borei p'ri ha-adamah. (Fruits and vegetables of the ground)

בָּרוּךְ אַתָּה יי אֱלֹהֵינוּ מֶלֶךְ הָעוֹלָם בּוֹרֵא פְּרִי הָעֵץ.

Barukh Attah Adonai, Eloheinu Melekh ha-Olam Borei p'ri ha-etz. (Fruits from trees)

GAME/MOVEMENT: Play "fruit salad": Everyone sits in a circle. Prepare two pictures of each fruit (e.g., two pears, two apples, two watermelons, two bananas, two bunches of grapes. Teach the names of the fruits in Hebrew. Randomly hand out the pictures. The "announcer" calls out one fruit, "apples/ *tapuhim*". The two children holding that fruit, quickly stand up and switch places. Continue calling each fruit. At some point, say, Fruit Salad." What happens is that EVERYONE stands up, gets "all mixed up," and finds a NEW place.

Apples	*tapuhim*	תַּפּוּחִים
Pears	*agasim*	אַגָּסִים
Watermelon	*avati'ah*	אֲבַטִּיחַ
Grapes	*anavim*	עֲנָבִים
Oranges	*tapuzim*	תַּפּוּזִים
Pineapple	*ananas*	אֲנָנָס

Parashat Ki Tavo Family Discussion

(from *Morah, Morah, Teach Me Torah*)

Ki tavo means "when you enter." Where are the people getting ready to enter? (The land of Canaan.) Remember, Moshe was not allowed to enter the land but wanted everyone to know what to do when they get there. Only Moshe heard the voice of God, who told Moshe what God wanted the people to remember.

Moshe told the people to offer the first fruits picked in the Promised Land as a gift offering (*bikkurim*). Those first fruits are the most special. Then Moshe talked about all that had happened since they left Egypt. He particularly wanted everyone to remember what will happen if they don't do good deeds and follow the rules. Then he gathered the twelve tribes together and divided them into two groups. One group of six tribes went to the top of Mount Grizim and the other group went to the top of Mount Eval. The group on Mount Grizim would listen for the blessings, or the good deeds, and when they heard them, they would say "Amen." The group on Mount Eval listened for the curses, or things they could be punished for; then they would say "Amen."

Family Discussion Questions:

1. (Q) The parashah talks about the importance of the first fruits. What are some important firsts in your life? (A) First teeth, first day of school, the first word they spoke, etc.
2. (Q) What are some firsts in the Torah? (A) First day of creation: first Jew—Avraham; first people—Adam and H̲ava; first commandment—"I am the Eternal your God."
3. (Q) Name some things that you do that you get praised for, such as if you clean your room, you can have a playdate. And name something that you might get punished for.

NITZAVIM

Last week the tribes were divided onto Mount Grizim and Mount Eval, and the blessings and curses were read. This week we read Parashat Nitzavim. *Nitzvavim* means "you are standing." Moshe was saying goodbye to the people as they gathered and stood before the land of Canaan. He said to them, "You are standing here before God, and you will make a covenant or a promise to God. You will become the chosen people. The covenant was not only with the people in the past but for all the people today and in years to come. God said to 'choose life,' and to obey the commandments and follow the Torah; then you will be able to enjoy the land that was promised to our fathers: Avraham [Abraham], Yitzhak [Isaac] and Ya'akov [Jacob]."

These are the words that Moshe wanted everyone to remember. Even if you make a mistake, God will forgive you if you do *t'shuvah*—ask for forgiveness.

We have learned that everyone, even children, are capable of studying and understanding Torah, just like we are doing now.

The Torah teaches us that laws are not too hard to learn. "They are in your heart and in your mouth." What do you think that means?

MULTIMEDIA IDEAS

"ASK ME" STICKER: Ask me what happens if I make a mistake.

LANGUAGE: Talk about what it means when God says, "The laws are in your heart and in your mouth."

GAME: God wants us all to do mitzvot. Play "Goofy Mitzvot" (גּוּף guf means "body" in Hebrew). On poster board, draw a large person. Place Velcro dots on the mouth (*peh*), nose (*af*), eyes (*einayim*), ears (*oznayim*), and hands (*yadayim*).

Have picture and/or word cards with a variety of mitzvot. Talk about which part of your body (*guf*) you use to do each mitzvah, and pin them onto the appropriate body parts, for example

Mouth: Eat h̲allah, speak kind words, eat apples and honey, eat kosher food, sing prayers.

Nose: Smell a *besamim* (spice) for *havdalah*, smell the *etrog* and fruits in the sukkah.

Eyes: Look at a Torah, look at Hebrew letters, watch the candles burning.

Ears: Hear a shofar being blown, hear the noise of a grogger, listen to Hebrew prayers and songs, the jingling of *rimonim* (Torah crowns).

Hand: Touch or hold the Torah, kiss a Mezuzah, light Shabbat candles, hold a *yad* to read Torah.

SONG (tune: "If You're Happy and You Know It"—traditional)

If you like to give *tzedakah*, clap your hands. (2x)
Use your *yadayim*, put *tzedakah* in the can.
If you like to give *tzedakah*, clap your hands.

If you can run to do a mitzvah, stomp your feet. (2x)
Use your *kof rag'layim* and run to help a friend.
If you can run to do a mitzvah, stomp your feet.

If you like to eat h̲allah, shout hooray! (2x)
Wash your *yadayim* and say a *brakhah* with your *peh.*
If you like to eat h̲allah, shout hooray!

If you can do Goofy Mitzvot, do all three (clap, stomp, hooray!). (2x)
We do mitzvot every day, and use our *guf* in many ways.
If you can do Goofy Mitzvot, do all three.

BOOK: *All About Me* by Dina Rosenfeld.

Parashat Nitzavim Family Discussion

(from *Morah, Morah, Teach Me Torah*)

Nitzavim means "you are standing." The people were standing in front of the land of Canaan, and Moshe was saying good-bye to them before they go. He said to them, "You are standing here before God, and you will make a covenant or promise to God. You will become "the chosen people." This covenant will last forever. Whoever chooses life and chooses to obey the commandments and follows the Torah will be able to enjoy the land that was promised to our fathers, Avraham, Yitzhak, and Ya'akov (Abraham, Isaac, and Jacob). Moshe reminded them that even if they make a mistake, God will forgive them if they ask for forgiveness—do *t'shuvah* and learn from their mistakes. Studying Torah is not hard to do. We are doing it now! The words of the Torah are "in our hearts and in our mouths."

Family Discussion Questions:

1. (Q) What do you think God meant by "the words of the Torah are in your heart and in your mouth"?
2. (Q) What kinds of mitzvot can you do?
3. (Q) What are the names of the fathers of the Jewish people from Torah? (A) Avraham, Yitzhak, and Ya'akov. (Q) Can you also name the mothers? (A) Sarah, Rivka, Rachel, and Leah.

VA-YELEKH

In last week's parashah we were reminded to study the Torah. We learned that we are the "chosen people." This week, we read Va-Yelekh, which means "and he went." Moshe went and spoke to the people. We're getting close to the end of the Torah.

Moshe was 120 years old! He knew he will soon die. He told Yehoshua (Joshua), "Be brave, be strong! *Hazak, hazak v'nit-hazek*!" (Do you remember hearing that before? Of course, we hear it each time we finish reading a book of the Torah!) Yehoshua will lead the people into Canaan, the Promised Land, and he will be the new leader of the Jewish people.

Moshe finished writing down all the laws and teachings from God. He gave the laws (the Torah) to the *Kohanim* to put into the ark in the *Mishkan*. These writings are the same words that are in our Torahs today. They are the same words that God spoke to Moshe.

SONG (tune: "Torah Tzevah Lanu Moshe"—traditional)

Torah (7x) is a gift from God.
Torah (7x) is a gift from God.
Torah (5x) is a gift from God.
Torah (5x) is a gift from God.

Moshe had been a good, strong leader for a long time, but now it was Yehoshua's turn to lead. Moshe told the people, "Don't be afraid; God is with you!"

MULTIMEDIA IDEAS

"ASK ME" STICKER: Ask me who the new leader for the Jewish people is. (Yehoshua.)

GAME: Play "Follow the leader." Or play "*Yehoshua Omer*" (Joshua says), like "Simon Says" but with Yehoshua's name instead.

CRAFT: Moshe finished writing the Torah. Take a roll of butcher paper and make your own Torah. Write/draw your favorite story that was in the Torah. You can use a feather and paint again like a sofer if you'd like.

PROJECT: We learned that writing or helping to write a Torah is a mitzvah. Fulfill that mitzvah by buying a letter in a sefer Torah in Israel: www.kidstorah.org. It only costs $1.00 (U.S. currency) per child under the age of twelve.

BOOK: *The Sefer Torah Parade* by Tzivia Adler.

LANGUAGE: Moshe tells Yehoshua, "*Hazak, hazak v'nit-hazek*—be brave and be strong." Talk about times that you were brave or times that you were scared, and write them down.

Parashat Va-Yelekh Family Discussion

(from *Morah, Morah, Teach Me Torah*)

Va-yelekh means "and he went"; Moshe went and spoke to the Jewish people. Moshe was 120 years old, and he knows he will soon die. He tells Yehoshua (Joshua), the new leader, be brave and strong—*Hazak, hazak, v'nit-hazek.*" Do you remember these words? We say them each time we finish reading a book of the Torah. Moshe finished writing down all the laws and the teachings from God. He gave the laws (the Torah) to the *Kohanim* to put in the ark in the *Mishkan*. These writings are the same words that are in our Torah today. Moshe had been a good and strong leader, but now it was Yehoshua's turn to lead. Moshe told the people, "Don't be afraid; God is with you."

Family Discussion Questions:

1. (Q) Do you think that Moshe was sad that he could not go into Canaan with the rest of the people?
2. (Q) Talk about a time when you were very brave and strong.
3. (Q) Do you remember what the *Mishkan* is? (A) The traveling shul where the laws were kept.
4. (Q) Where do we keep the Torah today? (A) In the *Aron ha-Kodesh*, the Ark.

HA'AZINU

In last week's parashah we learned about Moshe telling Yehoshua to be brave and to be strong (*hazak, hazak v'nit-hazek*) as he led *B'nai Yisrael* into the Promised Land of Canaan.

This week's parashah is called Ha'azinu, which means "listen" or "give ear to." In this parashah Moshe recited a poem called the "Song of Ha'azinu." The poem is all about God and the land Canaan (now called Israel). Moshe reminded the Jewish people to be good in the land "flowing with milk and honey [Canaan], to remember not to pray to idols and not to become spoiled and selfish or the face of God will turn away from us."

SONG: "Eretz Zavat Halav" (Israeli traditional song by Eliyahu Gamliel and dance—Land Flowing with Milk and Honey).

Shlock Rock has a cute version of this song on the CD *Shlock Rock for Kids Party Time!*

Eretz zavat halav, ooh, aah, halav u'd'vash. (4x)
Eretz zavat halav, zavat halav u'd'vash.
Eretz zavat halav, zavat halav u'd'vash.
(Repeat as many times as you like.)

Moshe reminded the people that the "Torah is a tree of life to those who hold fast to it, and its ways are the way to happiness." Moshe instructed the people to remember to teach the laws of the Torah to their children and to their children's children forever!

SONG: "Tree of Life" by Cantor Richard Silverman

It's a tree of life to them that hold fast to it,
and all its supporters are happy. (2x)

Shalom, shalom (clap, clap, clap, clap) shalom, shalom (clap, clap, clap, clap), shalom, shalom (clap 10 times fast).
Etz hayyim hi l'mahazikim bah
V'tom'khekha m'ushar. (2x)

(Repeat "Shalom" part.)

Moshe reminded *B'nai Yisrael* to have faith and trust in God.

Then God tells Moshe to climb to the top of Mount Nevo, where he can see the holy land of Canaan.

MULTIMEDIA IDEAS

"ASK ME" STICKER: Ask me what the "tree of life" is.

COOKING/SCIENCE: God described Canaan as a land flowing with milk and honey (*halav u'd'vash*).

1) Make a honey cake.

Honey Cake

2 cups flour
3/4 cup sugar
1 teaspoon cinnamon
3/4 cup honey
1/2 cup oil
2 eggs
1 teaspoon baking powder dissolved in 1/2 cup orange juice
1 teaspoon vanilla
1/4 cup sugar
1 teaspoon cinnamon

Combine all ingredients (except the additional cinnamon and sugar) in a bowl. Mix well. Preheat oven to 325 degrees. Pour half of the batter in a pan (sprayed with non-stick spray or greased), and sprinkle half of the cinnamon and sugar over the batter. Pour the rest of the batter and sprinkle the top with the remaining cinnamon and sugar.

Bake for 1 hour. Cake will rise as it bakes, so make sure there is enough room in the pan. Yum!

2) Make *g'lidah*—ice cream Put the following into a sandwich-sized Zip-Loc bag and "zip" closed:
1 tablespoon sugar, 1/2 cup milk or half-and-half,
1/4 teaspoon vanilla.

In a gallon-sized Zip-Loc bag put 2 tablespoons rock salt (baking aisle in grocery stores) and ice cubes to fill the bag about 3/4 full. Add the filled and zipped sandwich bag containing the milk mixture. Ziplock closed and shake and roll the filled bag over and over until frozen (about 15–20 min.)

As the ice melts it does leak a little, so do outside!

LANGUAGE: Moshe recites a poem in this week's parashah. Talk about poems. Work on rhyming words. Read some poems (Shel Silverstein, Robert Frost; even David Melekh Yisrael was a poet!). Are songs poems? Try writing a poem together as a group.

Examples:

Once there was a world created for me and you,
But we needed to get some rules, to tell us what to
_________(do).

Up to Mount Sinai, Moshe did go,
So God could tell him all we need to _________ (know).

Remembering these laws is not hard for me and you,
They are all about kindness and the things we ought to
_________ (do).

Once we were slaves and now we are free.
The Torah is a gift for you and _________. (ME!)

God said to be kind, God said to be good.
Follow all the Torah's laws, they way that we _________
(should).

CRAFT: Make a mural showing what you think a land flowing with milk and honey would look like. Use a variety of medium. Then look at actual pictures of Israel. How do they compare?

BOOK: *And Shira Imagined* by Giora Carmi.

GEOGRAPHY: Can you find Mount Nevo on your floor map of Israel?

Parashat Ha'azinu Family Discussion

(from *Morah, Morah, Teach Me Torah*)

Ha'azinu means "listen" or "give ear to." In this parashah Moshe recites a poem called the "Song of Ha'azinu." The poem is about God and the land of Canaan. Today Canaan is called Israel. Moshe reminded the Jewish people to be good in "the land flowing with milk and honey," to remember not to pray to idols and not to become spoiled or selfish or the face of God would turn away from them. There is a saying that says, "The Torah is a tree of life to those who hold fast to it [for those who believe in it] and its ways are the way to happiness." Moshe instructed the people to remember to teach the laws of the Torah to their children and their children's children forever. Then God told Moshe to climb to the top of Mount Nevo, where he could see the holy land of Canaan.

Family Discussion Questions:

1. (Q) Moshe writes a poem. Can you find a book that has poems in it to share? Are songs poems?
2. (Q) What do you think it means that the Torah is a tree of life?
3. (Q) Do you know the song by Cantor Richard Silverman called "Tree of Life"? Sing it with your family.

V'ZOT HA-BRAKHAH

This is the last parashah in the last book of the Torah. It is always a little sad when you finish reading a really good book. But we know the Torah goes in a circle, and its cycle never really ends. We get to start all over again at Bereshit!

This is Parashat V'zot ha-Brakhah, which means "this is the blessing." In this parashah, Moshe gave his final blessings to *B'nai Yisrael*. Moshe told the people that God loves them because they promised to follow the Torah. At Mount Sinai, the people said, "All that God says, we will do!"

There is a special song we sing when we take out the Torah.

SONG: "Torah Tzivah Lanu Moshe" (Israeli traditional)

Torah, Torah, Torah, Torah, Torah, Torah, Torah, tzivah lanu Moshe. (2x)
Torah, Torah, Torah, Torah, Torah tzivah lanu Moshe. (2x)
Morashah kehillat Ya'akov, (3x)
Torah tzivah lanu Moshe.

(The Torah commanded to Moshe belongs to us, the community of Ya'akov.)

Moshe blessed each of the twelve tribes and he had a special blessing for each tribe.

God showed Moshe the Promised Land of Canaan from the top of Mount Nevo. Moshe looked at the beautiful land that God promised to Avraham, Yitzhak and Ya'akov. Moshe then died. God buried him in a special secret place. Even today, we don't know where that place is. It is a very sad time for the Jewish people. They cried and prayed for thirty days. No other prophet (a special messenger from God) will ever be like Moshe. Only Moshe ever knew God face to face.

Just as we do at the end of each book of the Torah, we say: "*Hazak, hazak, v'nit-hazek*! Be strong, be strong, and be strengthened!"

SONG (tune: "Mary had a Little Lamb"—traditional)

Hazak, Hazak, v'nit-hazek, v'nit-hazek, v'nit-hazek.
Hazak, Hazak, v'nit-hazek—be brave and be strong.

We read five books of the Torah, the Torah, the Torah.
We read five books of the Torah and then we say *hazak.*

Now we finished Devarim, Devarim, Devarim.
Now we finished Devarim and so we say *hazak.*

Hazak, Hazak, v'nit-hazek, v'nit-hazek, v'nit-hazek.
Hazak, Hazak, v'nit-hazek—be brave and be strong.

MULTIMEDIA IDEAS

"ASK ME" STICKER: Ask me what happens when we finish reading the whole Torah.

LANGUAGE: Learn the song: *Torah tzivah lanu Moshe morasha kehillat Ya'akov* (The Torah commanded to Moshe belongs to us, the community of Ya'akov).

GAME: The Torah's cycle goes in a circle. Play circle games: Ahshav; Duck, Duck, Goose; and Ring around the Torah:

SONG: (tune: "Ring Around the Rosie"—traditional)

Ring around the Torah
Teach us, teach us, *morah*
Torah, Torah,
We all learn more.

CRAFT: Make a circle chart with the months of the year (English and/or Hebrew) out of poster board. (Divide it like a pie). Decorate each month with whatever holiday goes in that month (Tishrei—Rosh ha-Shanah, Yom Kippur, etc.). Make an arrow pointer attached with a paper fastener, and set it accordingly.

SONG: (tune: "Ain't It Great To Be Crazy?"—traditional)

Boom-boom ain't it great to read Torah
Boom-boom ain't it great to read Torah
Mitzvot, and stories the whole year through
Boom-boom ain't it great to read Torah.
(alternate: Boom boom it's so great to read Torah)

SONG: (tune: "*Oseh Shalom Bimromav*"—traditional)

Oh say shalom to Moshe
He was our very special leader
We'll enter Canaan without Moshe,
Without Moshe, without Moshe.

Let's all say shalom (shalom) (2x)
Shalom to Moshe
Canaan is our new home.

Let's all say shalom (shalom) (2x)
Shalom to Moshe
Canaan is our new home.

Parashat V'zot ha-Brakhah Family Discussion

(from *Morah, Morah, Teach Me Torah*)

This is the very last parashah in the last book of the Torah. It took us a long, long time to read the whole Torah—a whole year! Soon it will be time to start all over again at the beginning (Bereshit). Like with any really good book, we want to read it over and over again. *V'zot ha-brakhah* means "and these are the blessings." Moshe blessed each of the twelve tribes with a special blessing. God showed Moshe the Promised Land of Canaan from the top of Mount Nevo. Moshe looked at the land God promised to Avraham, Yitzhak and Ya'akov. Moshe then died and was buried in a special place. Only God knows where Moshe is buried. It was a very sad time for the Jewish people, yet it was also a happy time because they would now have a home they could call their own. Just as we do at the end of each book, we say "*Hazak, hazak v'nit-hazek! Be strong, and be strengthened.*" But our study of the Torah will not end here. We will always learn from it again, and again, forever. Amen!

Family Discussion Questions:

1. (Q) How do you feel when you finish reading a favorite book?
2. (Q) We sing this song in synagogue: "*Torah tzivah lanu Moshe.*" Do you know when we sing this song? (A) When the Torah is lifted up high after it has been read. (Q) Can you sing the song now?
3. (Q) Can you think of your favorite Torah story (parashah) you have learned about?

ROSH HODESH

Rosh Hodesh means "the head of the month" (just like Rosh Ha-Shanah means "the head of the year"). When a new moon appears in the sky, we know the month has ended. A new moon is actually when the moon is not visible in the sky at all. When a crescent moon appears in the sky, we know it is Rosh Hodesh, or the start of a new Hebrew month. It is a mitzvah to celebrate Rosh Hodesh; we learned about it in parashat Bo.

In ancient times, people didn't have calendars; they relied on the sun and moon to tell time. The sun was used in the day to tell what time of day it was, based on where the sun was in the sky. The moon was used to tell when a month was over and when a new month started, so we would know when holidays were. Remember how many times God asked us to remember to keep Shabbat, to celebrate Sukkot, Pesah, and Shavuot? It was very important to know when those holidays were! We could tell what part of the month it was by how the moon looked. At the beginning of a new month, there is a moon shaped like a crescent. After a while, there's a half moon, then there's a full, round moon (that's the middle of the month—usually the fifteenth of the Hebrew month), and then it starts getting smaller until it disappears. That's when the month is over.

Whenever at least two people saw the crescent moon in the sky, a shofar was sounded. Then the word was sent out that it was a new month. There were special prayers said and special gift offerings to God on Rosh Hodesh. Even today, we say special prayers called *Hallel*. It was customary for the women to rest on Rosh Hodesh as their reward for not participating in the golden calf (see parashat Ki Tissa). Even today, some women get together to celebrate Rosh Hodesh. So watch the sky for that crescent moon and get your shofar ready!

MULTIMEDIA IDEAS

"ASK ME" STICKER: Ask me how you can tell if it is a new Hebrew month.

ACTIVITY: At the start of a new month, have a Rosh Hodesh party! Blow the shofar! Decorate T-shirts to wear each month on Rosh Hodesh. Have this be a special time when the children can share things with the class and have special self-reflection time. Make a special moon-shaped snack to eat (bread and cheese cut into a crescent shape; crescent rolls, make pretzels and shape them like the moon, apple slices, etc.). Sing special Rosh Hodesh songs, and teach the names of the Hebrew months (see below and Parashah Aharei Mot), and read special moon-related stories (see below). Decorate your room so the kids know when they come into the room that it is Rosh Hodesh!

CRAFT: 1) Make a phases of the moon picture or chart. Cut out a circle from poster board and draw the different cycles of the moon (crescent, half moon, full moon, half moon, crescent, no moon) or cut them out of paper). Make an arrow attached with a paper fastener to point to the correct phase. Make sure you pay attention—it changes weekly! At the start of a new month have a Rosh Hodesh party!

2) With black paper, make a picture of a Rosh Hodesh moon, and decorate the paper with stars and glitter, etc. Label the picture with the name of the new month. Teach the names of the Hebrew months (see the song in Parashat Aharei Mot).

3) Paint with moon and star stampers.

4) Take a piece of black paper and cut a slit in the center of it the long way. Cut out a circle from yellow paper and attach it with a paper fastener at the slit. Slide the moon in and out of the slit to show the phases of the moon. Decorate the paper with stars and glitter, etc.

COOKING: Make moon-shaped cookies. See the sugar cookie recipe in Parashah Bereshit.

GAME: Practice moon and star sequencing.

Make a few crescent moon shapes out of poster board, attach yarn, and punch holes in the sides to create lace-ups.

SCIENCE: Take a paper cup and poke holes onto the bottom in a design (Magen David, crescent moon). With a flashlight, shine the light through the cup in a darkened room.

PROJECT: 1) Create a Rosh Hodesh book with the phases of the moon for your bookshelf. Have each child draw a page and create the story.

2) Each Rosh Hodesh, have the children draw a self-portrait, and keep the drawings to observe their progress. Send them all home at the end of the year to share each Rosh Hodesh's progress.

SONG (tune: "Oh, Mr. Sun, Sun, Mr. Golden Sun"— traditional with adaptations by the authors.)

Oh Mr. Moon, Moon, Mr. Golden Moon,
Please shine down on me.
Oh Mr. Moon, Moon, Mr. Golden Moon,
What do you look like, please?
It's Rosh Hodesh, a new month too.
You look like a sliver, our little moon.
Oh Mr. Moon, Moon, Mr. Golden Moon,
Please shine down on me.

SONG (tune: "You Are My Sunshine"by Jimmie Davis and Charles Mitchell, with adaptations by the authors)

You are my crescent moon, my little crescent moon
You make me happy it's Rosh Hodesh
It's a new month now, a new Hebrew month
Oh I love my Rosh Hodesh moon!

SONG (tune: "Matchmaker" by Jerry Bock, with adaptations by the authors)

Rosh Hodesh, Rosh Hodesh
It's a new month, a sliver moon, a new Hebrew month.
Rosh Hodesh, Rosh Hodesh
What's the new month...
It's the Hebrew month ______________.

BOOKS: While these are not about Rosh Hodesh, they are about moons and they are cute:

When the Moon Smiled, a math and counting book by Petr Horacek

Good Night Moon by Margaret Wise Brown.

Papa, Please Get the Moon For Me by Eric Carle.

Moonbeam Bear by Rolf Fanger and Ulrike Moltgen.

Why the Moon Only Glows by Dina Rosenfeld.

Bibliography

Berman, Melanie, and Joel Lurie Grishaver. *My Weekly Sidrah.* Los Angeles: Torah Aura Productions, 1986.

Chabara, Yona, Miriam Feinberg, and Rena Rotenberg. *Torah Talk.* Denver: Alternatives in Religious Education, 1989.

Etz Hayim: Torah and Commentary. Edited by David L. Lieber. Philadelphia: Jewish Publications Society, 2001.

Loeb, Sorel Goldberg, and Barbara Binder Kadden. *Teaching Torah: A Treasury of Insights and Activities.* Denver: Alternatives in Religious Education, 1997.

Newman, Shirley. *A Child's Introduction to Torah*: New York: Behrman House, 1954.

Prenzlau, Sheryl. *Deuteronomy: The Jewish Children's Bible.* New York: Pitspopany Press, 1998.

Peterseili, Gedalia. *Tell It from the Torah*: NY, Jerusalem: Pitspopany Press, 1997.

Prenszlau, Sheryl. *Exodus: The Jewish Children's Bible.* New York: Pitspopany Press, 1998.

Prenazlau, Sheryl. *Genesis: The Jewish Children's Bible.* New York: Pitspopany Press, 1998.

Prenzlau, Sheryl. *Leviticus: The Jewish Children's Bible.* New York: Pitspopany Press, 1998.

Prenzlau, Sheryl. *Numbers: The Jewish Children's Bible.*New York: Pitspopany Press, 1998.

Samuels, Ruth. *Bible Stories for Jewish Children.* New York: Ktav Publishing House, 1954.

Saypol, Judith-Wikler, Madeline. *My Very Own Haggadah.* Silver Spring MD: Kar-Ben Publishing, 1974.

Weissman, R. *My First Parasha Reader.* Brooklyn NY: B'nay Yakov Publications, 1993.

Music Resources

Shirley R. Cohen, Kinor Records (1951).

Judy Caplan Ginsburgh, board member of Pickleberry Pie, Inc., www.judymusic.com.

Greg and Steve, *Kids in Motion* CD, www.gregandsteve.com.

Kar-Ben Publishing, *My Very Own Haggadah* (1974), www.karben.com.

Carol Boyd Leon, *Gan Shirim,* www.carolboydleon.com.

Irene Light, board member of Pickleberry Pie, Inc. www.childrensmusic.org or www.lightmotifs.com.

Jill Moskowitz, jillsm@aol.com.

Cantor Richard Silverman *Cantor Richard Silverman Song Book*, www.soundswrite.com.

Lenny Solomon of Shlock Rock, www.shlockrock.com.

Uncle Moishe, www.unclemoishe.com.

About the Authors

Tobey Greenberg and Nechama Retting live in the Washington, D.C. Metropolitan area.

Tobey has been a Jewish early childhood educator for over twenty-three years. She taught for thirteen years at a Jewish Community Center and is currently teaching at a congregational preschool, where she has taught for over six years. She taught the three-year-old class for three years and is currently teaching the pre-K class. Tobey also has a wonderful husband and two children.

Nechama has been an early childhood educator and has taught at a congregational preschool for more than thirteen years and has taught religious school for over nine years. She was the director of a Camp Gan Israel for nine years. She teaches a three-year-old class and a two-year-old class. Nechama also has a wonderful husband and five children.

Working together at their preschool, the authors participate in a very special *Kabbalat Shabbat* program each week. The rabbi leads the children in Shabbat and holiday songs, and then the authors take the children back to biblical times, where they have an opportunity to act out the stories written in our Torah. Each week, as we prepare for Shabbat, the children reenact the Torah portion through drama, stories, songs, and activities. The children have so much fun reliving the Torah that Tobey and Nechama decided to compile all of these stories into one book so that others could make the Torah an active part of their children's lives.

Contact the authors at: Torah4kids@gmail.com.

Visit our Web site at www.Torah4kids.com.

Notes

Notes

Notes

Notes

Notes

Notes

Notes

Notes

Notes